35 Best walks around Marbella
Discover mountains, lakes, white villages, heritage & their stories

Saskia Meulemans

© Saskia Meulemans 2021

The rights of Saskia Meulemans to be identified as the author of this work have been asserted by her in accordance with the Copyright, Designs and Patents Act of 1988.

All rights reserved; no part of this publication may be reproduced, stored in a retrieval system, or transmitted in any form or by any means, electronic, mechanical, photocopying, recording or otherwise without the prior written consent of the publisher or a licence permitting copying in the UK issued by the Copyright Licensing Agency Ltd. www.cla.co.uk

ISBN 978-1-78222-883-7

Book design, layout and production management by Into Print
intoprint.net
Edited by: Etheridiom.net

Photographs
Saskia Meulemans

Cover photo
El Chorro, Ronda, Casares, Marbella

Maps
Openstreetmap.org and freecountrymaps.com and wikiloc.com

Disclaimer
Every effort has been made to achieve accuracy of information for use in this guidebook. The author and publisher can take no responsibility or liability for any loss (including fatal), damage or trespass as a result of the route information or advice offered in this guidebook.

The inclusion of a path or track in this guide does not guarantee it remains a right of way. If conflict with a land owner occurs, please leave by the shortest possible route available and inform the relevant authority if deemed necessary.

Please follow the country code and always give way to pedestrians and horses.

For my boys

CONTENTS

Preface 8
Introduction 10
How to use this book. 14
Important information 16
Table of walks. 18
Overview maps 20

PART 1 Marbella: Introduction 23
Part 1.1   Marbella Coastal Paths: blue sea with history . . 29
Walk 1   Dunes & watchtowers: Cabopino to Mijas 33
Walk 2   From old Marbella to jet-set Marbella: Los Monteros, the centre & the Golden Mile walk . 39
Walk 3   Puerto Banús to San Pedro: wooden bridges and archaeological sites 51
Part 1.2   True mountain feel on your doorstep: the Sierra Blanca 61
STARTING POINT NAGUELES PARK
Walk 4   The old mining forest trail of Buenavista 67
Walk 5   Stunning lake view walk from Marbella to Istán village 73
STARTING POINT DON MIGUEL/TRAPICHE
Walk 6   Monks, waterfalls and coastal views: the 'Monjes' walk. 83
Walk 7   Marbella´s viewpoint peak: the 'Gitanos' walk . 89
STARTING POINT PUERTO RICO/LA CAÑADA
Walk 8   Gorgeous cliffs, river and views: the Lighthouse trail 95
Walk 9   Children's mountain circuit up Tajo Travertino 101
Walk 10 Marbella to the white village of Ojén 107
Walk 11 Straight up to the viewpoint terrace Montés of Juanar. 113
STARTING POINT: UP ON THE MOUNTAIN AT JUANAR
Walk 12 Olive trees, pine forest and climb to the peak of La Cruz. 119

Walk 13	For hiking experts: a not-to-be missed hike up to the peak of La Concha 125
Walk 14	From high up in Juanar down to Marbella promenade: valleys & views. 131

PART 2 White mountain villages close to Marbella: Ojén, Monda, Istán and Benahavis. 136

Part 2.1	Ojén: from authentic village to international fame 139
Walk 15	Ojén village to the El Corzo viewpoint 143
Part 2.2	Monda: panoramic views to Sierra Nevada . . 150
Walk 16	Viewpoints at the Holy Cave and La Canucha. 153
Part 2.3	Istán: an important water source for the coast . 158
Walk 17	Istán's magic reservoir & chapel: Camino de la Cuesta 163
Walk 18	Spectacular viewpoints of Istán. 169
Walk 19	Water fun at the rockpools of the Charco del Canalón. 175
Part 2.4.	Benahavis: gastronomic gem 180
Walk 20	Benahavis lake, mountain and Montemayor castle 185
Walk 21	Benahavis: Arab irrigation channels and river walk 191

PART 3 Spectacular nature and beautiful sites a little further away 196

3.1.	DIRECTION RONDA & NORTH OF RONDA
Walk 22	Sierra de las Nieves National Park: La Torrecilla peak 201
Walk 23	Down Ronda's spectacular gorge: a taste of history and wine. 207
Walk 24	From Roman Acinipo to the cave houses of Setenil de las Bodegas. 217
Walk 25	Cat's cave mountain circuit near Benaoján 225

	Chestnut paradise: the Valle del Genal............. 233
Walk 26	From Cartajima to the Smurf village of Júzcar. 237
Walk 27	Chestnut route: Igualeja-Parauta............ 243
3.2.	DIRECTION ESTEPONA & INLAND
Walk 28	Award-winning art and hills of the Genalguacil 'Museo Pueblo' 251
Walk 29	Canyon of the vultures: Alcornocales Park... 257
Walk 30	Majestic cliff village of Casares: Crestellina mountain views and summit walk 263
Walk 31	The red Sierra de Bermeja and the unique Spanish fir tree: to the 'Los Reales' peak 271
3.3	DIRECTION MÁLAGA-ANTEQUERA
Walk 32	Mijas panoramic mountain circuit including the Puerto de Málaga peak 279
Walk 33	Cone-shaped rock labyrinth of El Torcal Natural Park................... 287
	El Chorro: magic reservoirs, gorge and Caminito del Rey. 292
Walk 34	Caminito del Rey: spectacular canyon thrill .. 295
Walk 35	El Chorro. Lake views' walk: El Gaitanejo ... 301

BIBLIOGRAPHY 304

PREFACE

There is so much more to Marbella than sun, beaches, shopping, and exquisite paella! Nearby, there are spectacular mountains to hike, picturesque villages to explore, and exciting legends, stories and history to be discovered. After years of walking in Málaga Province, I've still only seen a fraction of what is out there. The list is endless. New archaeological sites are being excavated and new pathways are being built on the coast and in the mountains. Wherever my feet take me, there is always a new story or another trail that crosses my path. I'd probably have to live a few more life-times to hike them all and research their hidden cultural or natural treasures. And I'm only talking about all there is within around 1.5-hours drive from Marbella.

This is what I would like to share with you: a careful and varied selection of the most exciting walks for all levels. Friends regularly ask me for directions to villages, which walks to do, or places to visit. They've never heard of or been to some of these places, and many of them have lived here for longer than me. Their requests aren't surprising though, as it takes a lot of time, effort, and a sense of adventure to search routes, try them out (get lost and frustrated!), and select the best. This book has been written for them and for anyone who lives here or comes to visit this beautiful part of southern Spain. But also for my children, who are growing up here and have often seen their parents leave the house in hiking gear or accompanied us on some of the walks. I hope all of you will appreciate the walks and the stories related to them and find the itineraries easy to follow. A selection of more challenging walks has been added for experienced hikers, who can generally find their way around. I hope they (as well as those who can't join in on the hikes) enjoy learning about the stories of hikes. My intention is to make your walking experience more fun by highlighting a different theme, fact, or legend related to the rich cultural or natural heritage, or by just recounting a fun story.

This little book is my personal creative project, and I hope it sparks interest in getting out there, being in touch with nature, and feeling the same love, excitement, and gratitude that I do. Embrace the beauty that is all around this area. After all, life is about experiences!

Enjoy!

INTRODUCTION

The mountain ranges in and around Marbella in the province of Málaga are fantastic destinations for walkers of all levels. The diversity of landscapes is exciting, surprising, and will never bore you. There are stunning natural parks with invaluable ecosystems that include many fauna and flora as well as geological formations that are rarely found elsewhere. From Marbella alone, you can see a variety of mountain ranges. To the north are the Sierra Blanca and Sierra de las Nieves mountains, which, as I write, have just received protection as a national park. The mountain towards Estepona is the Sierra Bermeja, to the northwest you can see the Sierra Real and Serrania de Ronda, and to the east lies the Sierra de Mijas. Marbella is all the more interesting, enriching, and fun if you walk all the mountains you can see from the coast. Once your curiosity is sparked to discover more, there are endless possibilities not too far way, from magic Ronda to spectacular El Chorro.

The walks are excellent for your body and mind, and you'll not only bring back wonderful memories but also local delicacies, such as the most diverse olive oils, cheeses, wines, nuts, and more. These always taste better when you've bought them in the places where they were produced. In autumn, for example, when hot chestnuts are sold on Marbella´s street corners, it's nice to remember walking through the colourful chestnut landscapes of the Valle del Genal, where they were collected.

The mountain slopes are dotted with picturesque white villages that tell tales and stories of a rich cultural heritage. From cave houses to Roman ruins, from Arab to Christian art and architecture, the mountains are a vast museum covering thousands of years of history. All of this can be found within easy reach of the coast. After decades of construction by the sea, town councils are becoming increasingly aware of the importance of conservation. The remaining beach dunes have now been protected as valued eco-reserves with wooden footpaths that make them enjoyable for visitors. This unique mix of a rich cultural and natural heritage makes walking in this southern region of Spain truly wonderful.

A dive into the region's past ...

Walking the mountains and visiting the villages is partly about discovering the eventful history of Andalucía. Many wars were fought here and entire civilizations left indelible marks on all the sciences, art, customs, and architecture.

...from Arab to Catholic rulers

Andalucía's culture is saturated in the influence of the Arabs or Moors, who occupied Spain for centuries after their arrival in 711. They built towns and defensive fortifications creating a political-economic order which lasted for centuries. They also left behind the charming white-washed hamlets that dot the hills and mountains.

When the Catholic Kings took back power, they maintained the fortifications, destroyed some parts, and built churches or added Christian elements to the existing Moorish architecture. All this activity has given the towns and villages a very unique Andalucian character. From far away, you can see the white villages that are perched on mountain slopes and are surrounded by the most beautiful seemingly endless mountain ranges. This magical image captivates tourists, who come to visit from all over the world.

…on foundations laid by the Romans

The Iberian Peninsula is deeply rooted in the history of the Roman Empire. Andalucía was called Baetica at that time, and was of great importance as it was the gateway to the Mediterranean and Africa. In an ever-expanding Roman empire, the region flourished as it offered them everything from its strategic location to its climate. Also, the Romans must have felt extremely happy that the conditions for wine making were excellent in the area. If you want to discover this rich Roman heritage, there are many sites to visit including the more well-known and bigger ruins of Baelo Claudia Roman City in nearby Tarifa and the great amphitheatre in Málaga. But there are the many other smaller sites mentioned in this book, including Ronda´s best kept secret, the ancient city of Acinipo. Situated just outside Ronda, it has one of the best preserved Roman theatres in Spain and is surprisingly peaceful as there are few tourists. Beginning in the 20th century, and especially in recent years, more Roman sites have been discovered, excavated, and preserved for the future.

Hiking tourism

Increasingly, visitors are looking to complement their beach stays with something different and venture inland. Locals are also increasingly curious about the beautiful nature and heritage around them, but do not always know where to start or only find their way to the most popular sites close by. This is completely understandable. For this reason, this book acts as a guide to some of the best of these natural parks around Marbella within Málaga Province. It not only includes some classic walks, but also covers other less-known routes. Before exploring inland, it's good to get to know your own area and walk through the history of Marbella on the newer wooden footpaths and beach promenades. Town councils are making enormous efforts to clean, renovate, and add paths and install information panels with maps and signposts with numbered trails throughout the province. Up to only a few years ago, many paths were not indicated and it was quite an adventure to find and follow most of the walks. It's still not always easy to find a lot of the trails, and hopefully this book will make your explorations more pleasant.

There are only a limited number of walks that can be covered in any book. So, I present a careful and varied selection of 35 walks for every taste, season, and level. Many of the walks are in Marbella, on the Sierra Blanca mountain, and on the nearby Sierra de las Nieves. Some of the walks are further from Marbella, but an easy scenic drive will introduce you to a complete different landscape or unique site. These walks are half- or full-day excursions with a maximum driving time of 1.5 hours.

Healthy mind and body

At the time of writing, Spain and the rest of the world are confronted with a serious pandemic crisis and nobody knows what the outcome will be. People around the world are experiencing chaotic and continuous changes of rules to live by to fight a virus that is rapidly spreading. Without any doubt, walking in the mountains always boosts your immune system, enriches your mind, and strengthens your body, and it's needed more now than ever!

HOW TO USE THIS BOOK

Walking area covered

Marbella is the home base and all driving directions are from there. The driving distance from Marbella is carefully indicated so you can easily time your half- or full-day excursion (in fact, this is how this book started, I explored walks within the timeframe of my children´s school hours!). The area covered lies within Málaga Province: even so, there are endless hikes to choose from and a selection somehow had to be made. I describe more walks within the Marbella home base because people tend to stay in their area. The longer the drive, the more varied the theme of the walk and its heritage. This book is divided into three parts. The first part describes walks within the Marbella area and on the Sierra Blanca mountain. The second part suggests walks in the white villages within a 30-minute drive from Marbella. The third part presents some walks with interesting themes within a 1 to 1.5-hour drive: these walks are of unique natural and cultural interest, like the more well-known Caminito del Rey.

Level & Time

The issues of level and time can be very personal. The walks presented are for medium-level hikers walking at an easy pace. In fact, most of the suggested walks are easy or medium level, so everyone can enjoy visiting the precious natural and cultural heritage. Expert hikers will usually find their way and can use the guide to learn about places, or connect several walks described in this book to form a larger itinerary.

Elevation gain

The elevation gain of each walk is indicated under the heading "The Facts". Elevation gain indicates the altitude you gain when on the walk, but take note that it is not the highest point you will reach. This is a good indicator of the level of difficulty, because one path can almost go straight up without any descents, whereas another could run over several valleys with many steep ups and downs. In this case, you would climb a lot more than just the difference in altitude from your starting point to arrival.

Tip

I sometimes provide a tip at the end of the description of a walk. For example, some shorter walks can easily be connected to longer ones if desired. I also provide information on other walks in the area, but which have not been described as they fall outside the scope of this book.

History, stories and more

Every walk has its story and can be of any kind: it can highlight the cultural or natural heritage, or just be a fun or interesting fact. This makes the experience more entertaining and educational. The title of each walk is a guideline to what to expect.

Step-by-step walking guide

The itinerary is described using simple bullet points to ((hopefully!) make your way easy to find. For your convenience, you can combine the itineraries with the **wikiloc** map. Every walk has a wikiloc map giving you a rough idea about the geographical setting and the level of inclination. The maps printed in this book can be found under 'saskiam' in the wikiloc app, which you can download or follow in real time, whichever is more convenient.

IMPORTANT INFORMATION

GO PREPARED

The whole idea is to explore and enjoy, which means **careful preparation**. To my surprise, I keep seeing people on hikes with almost no **water** (or none at all!), unsuitable shoes, and asking for directions because they got lost. Plan your trip according to your health and physical ability, prevent heat stroke, and do not get lost. Bring your map, trail description, and mobile phone, check the weather forecast, and let someone know where you are going. Bring abundant **water** (1 litre per 1-hour hike), **energy food**, a **hat,** and **sunscreen**, and wear proper **hiking shoes** and carry **hiking sticks**. Never walk alone in the mountains and make sure friends and family are equally prepared.

TAKE RESPONSIBILITY

The routes described in this book, as well as the wikiloc app trails, are simply suggestions. It is the responsibility of whoever goes on a walk to take the appropriate safety measures. These will depend on, but are not limited to, the weather conditions, group members, changed or destroyed signposts, as well as the technical and physical preparation of the walker. At the time of writing, everything described (trail and comments) is based on my own best research and extensive walking experience. However, the descriptions are there to inform the reader and, as such, are merely informative and do not convey any other kind of encouragement. Thus, the author is absolved from any responsibility in the event of any mishap that may be experienced by whoever freely decides to go on the walks on their own initiative. Never get lost, watch your step, and return immediately if you are unsure of the direction to go.

FOLLOW THE WIKILOC APP

All walks are registered on wikiloc under 'saskiam'. Just search for the name of the hike you want to do and select 'follow' to follow the track in real time. The wikiloc app is a good and fun guide, but lacks detailed information on the path or the cultural and natural heritage and stories that go with it. Get familiar with the application and guidebook by going on a short walk before undertaking a harder or longer walk. All maps used in this book are downloaded from the wikiloc app with approval from the wikiloc company.

TABLE OF WALKS

WALK	NAME WALK	KM	HOURS	LEVEL
Part 1	Marbella Coastal Paths: blue sea with history			
1	Dunes & watchtowers: Cabopino to Mijas	10	2	easy
2	From old Marbella to jet-set: Los Monteros, centre Marbella & Golden Mile	14	2.5	easy
3	Puerto Banús to San Pedro wooden bridges and archeological sites	10.5	2.5	easy
4	The old mining forest trail of Buenavista	5.4	2.5	moderate
5	Stunning lake view walk from Marbella to Istán village	8.8	2.5	moderate
6	Monks, waterfalls and coastal views: the `Monjes´ walk	5.32	2.15	moderate
7	Marbella´s viewpoint peak: the `Gitanos´walk	4.12	2	moderate
8	Gorgeous cliffs, river and views `The lighthouse trail´	6.78	3	moderate
9	Childrens' mountain circuit up Tajo Travertino	3.65	1.5	easy
10	Marbella to the white village of Ojén	9.3	3	moderate
11	Straight up to the viewpoint terrace Montés of Juanár	11.26	4	moderate
12	Olive trees, pine forest and climb to the peak of La Cruz	6.15	2.5	moderate
13	For experts: not-to-miss hike up to the peak of La Concha	13.69	6	difficult
14	From high up in Juanár down to Marbella promenade: valleys & views	12	5	difficult
Part 2	White villages close to Marbella: Sierra de las Nieves			
15	Ojén village to the El Corzo viewpoint	11.23	4	moderate
16	Viewpoints at the Holy Cave & Canucha	13	3.5	moderate
17	Istáns´magic reservoir & chapel Camino de la Cuesta	5.86	2.20	moderate
18	Spectacular viewpoints of Istán	5	1.5	easy

WALK	NAME WALK	KM	HOURS	LEVEL
19	Waterfun at the rockpools of the Charco del Canalón	5	1.5	easy
20	Benahavis lake, mountain and Montemayor castle	10.3	3	moderate
21	Benahavis Arab water channels and river walk	7.7	1.5	easy
Part 3	Spectacular Natural Sites within 1.5hrs drive			
22	Sierra de las Nieves´ peak of Torrecilla	16.68	6	difficult
23	Down Ronda´s spectacular gorge: a taste of history and wine	8	2	easy
24	From Roman Acinipo to the cave houses of Setenil de las Bodegas	13	3.5	easy
25	Cat´s cave mountain circuit near Benaoján	7.89	2.5	moderate
26	From Cartajima to the Smurf village of Júzcar	8.58	2	easy
27	Chestnut route: Igualeja-Parauta	13.24	3.5	moderate
28	Award-winning art and hills of the Genalguacil 'Museo Pueblo'	5.72	1.5	easy
29	Canyon of the vultures: Alcornocales Park	10	3	easy
30	Majestic cliff village of Casares:Crestellina mountain views & summit	10.14	4	moderate
31	The red Sierra de Bermeja and the unique Spanish fir tree: to the 'Los Reales' peak	12.28	3.5	moderate
32	Mijas panoramic mountain circuit including the Puerto de Málaga peak	12	3.5	moderate
33	Cone-shaped rock labyrinth of El Torcal Natural Park	3.5	2	easy
34	Caminito del Rey: spectacular canyon thrill	6.36	2.5	easy
35	El Chorro. Lake views walk El Gaitanejo	6	2	easy

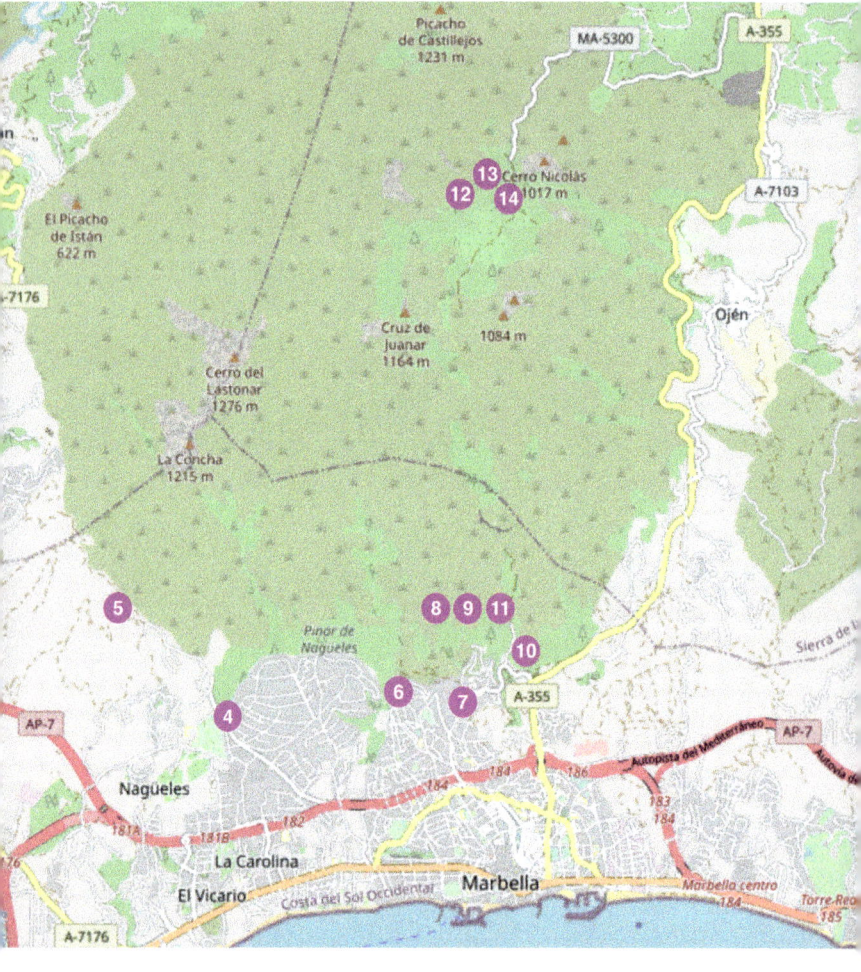

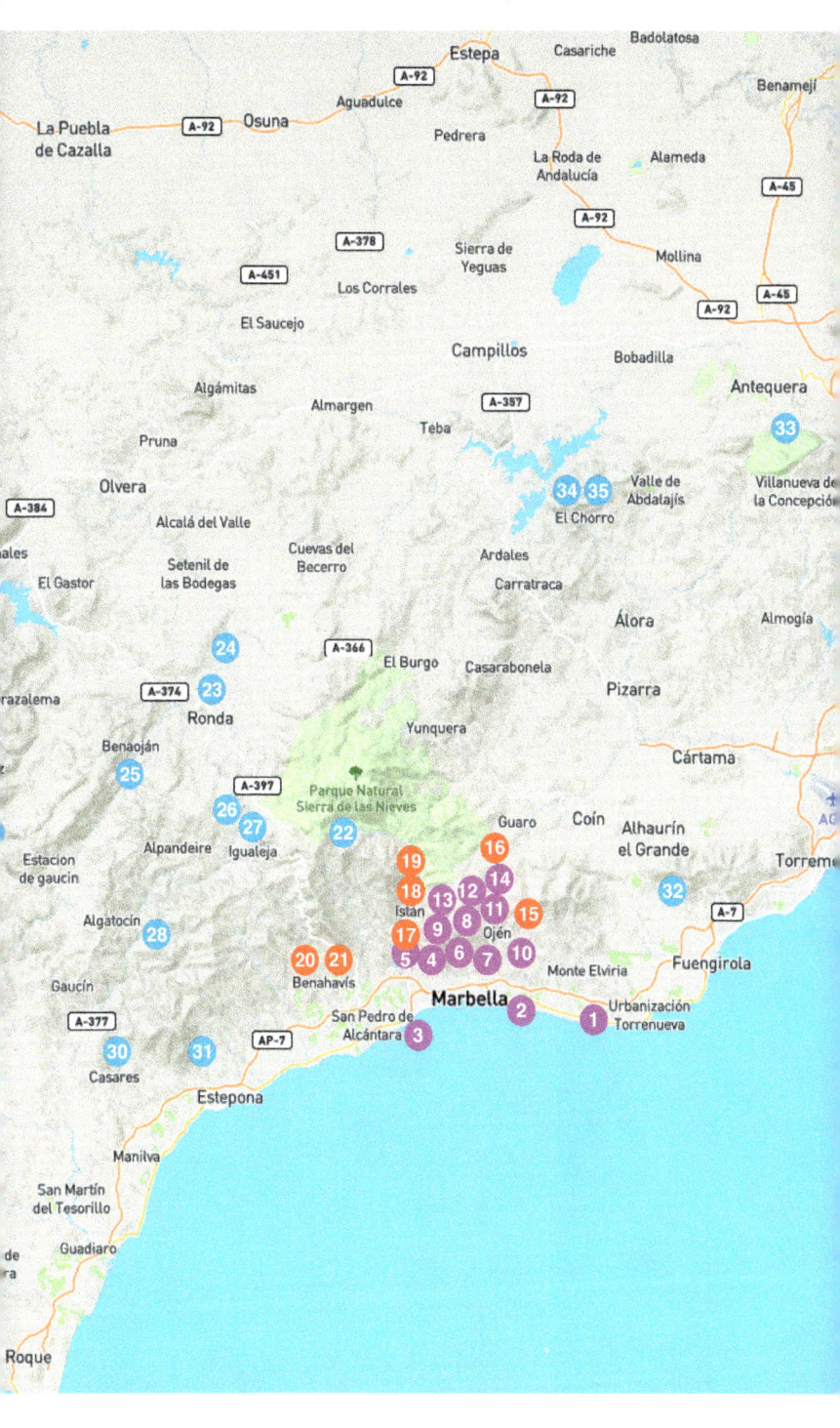

PART 1

Marbella: Introduction

Marbella is known as the indisputable chic and cosmopolitan seaside resort of the Costa del Sol, with high-end properties and top-notch facilities while remaining equally and truly authentic Andalucían. Thanks to protection from the nearby mountains, Marbella owes a lot to its fabulous climate with hot dry summers and pleasant winters, with no less than 320 sunny days per year and an average temperature of 19°C. Marbella is mostly associated with sun-drenched beaches, exclusive clubs and parties, luxury hotels, yacht-filled marinas, nightlife, exquisite dining, and many impeccable golf courses. Its rich cultural heritage and spectacular landscape of endless hills and mountain ranges are not necessarily the first things that come to mind, but they are the magic ingredients of this little paradise on earth, where people want to live or keep coming back. The colourful fusion of Spanish people and international residents from all corners of the world—who have chosen to settle here for longer or shorter periods—have made Marbella what it is today: a place of a million stories.

Bigger than you think

Situated in the province of Málaga, Marbella covers a coastal area of 117 square kilometres between Estepona and Mijas. It includes no less than five districts: Cabopino and east Marbella, Marbella centre, the Golden mile, Nueva Andalucia and Puerto Banus, and finally San Pedro de Alcántara. To the north it is bordered by the villages of Benahavis, Istán and Ojén and protected by the Sierra Blanca mountain, which is partly within the municipality. Around 147,000 inhabitants call it home and have access to several hospitals, many private clinics, numerous local and international schools, four yacht marinas, and many other facilities including endless shops, sports centres, clean beaches, restaurants, and much more. The best part is there's little to no traffic, no pollution, and all these wonderful facilities are within a couple of minutes' walk or short drive.

And if Marbella isn't big enough, you can hop over to the historical cities of Sevilla, Cordoba, or Granada, or go just around the corner to Málaga, a bustling city with a beautiful historic centre, a range of wonderful museums, and the bullet train to Madrid. Then there is Tarifa for kitesurfing, the Sierra Nevada for skiing, and the spectacular natural parks and mountains in the province, which you'll need a few lifetimes to explore. Only a litte further away, just under a 4-hours' drive, there's Portugal, where you can plunge into yet another a different culture and world.

Discover Marbella on foot

If you know Marbella well and are reasonably fit, you might have made your way up Juanar for a walk. But if you are just passing by, visiting, or even work here and haven't had a chance to explore it enough, you are hereby invited to go out, walk, and discover a part of the rich history this municipality has to offer. In recent years, monuments and natural enclaves, such as the dunes, are being gradually restored, protected, and opened to the public, and efforts have been made to make Marbella a greener town, highlight its biodiversity, and encourage healthy habits.

A little dive into Marbella's past...

"Oh! Que mar tan bella!", exclaimed the Catholic Queen Isabel after the conquest of Marbella on the 11th of June, 1485. This is how Marbella received its name... Such a lovely legend, but historians say that Marbella was actually the Castillian interpretation of the already similar Arab name 'Marbil-la'. The name alone reveals the intense history it has gone through with many different rulers claiming this territory. The entire culture, art, and architecture is drenched in Moorish and Catholic styles.

First settlements and Romans

Human activity in Marbella can be traced back as far as the Palaeolithic and Phoenician eras. The Phoenicians arrived some 2,700 years ago and boosted the local economy with the production and marketing of salted fish. The Romans later used this to create a special sauce, called garum, and exported this product throughout their entire Empire. Garum was made with olive oil and fermented fish. The archaeological sites of Roman life are highlighted on the coastal walks described in this book, including the Rio Verde Roman villa, the Palaeochristian basilicum, and the Roman baths.

Muslim occupation

In the 10th century, the Alcazaba (Fortress) of Marbella was built on the remains of a Roman settlement, giving birth to what we now call the Old Town of Marbella. Over time, it grew following the typical al-Andalus city model consisting of three parts: the walled city or medina, the citadel as a center of power, and the suburbs outside the walls. Today's Casco Antiguo (Old Town) was the heart of the Islamic town and protected by walls and towers. Some of the streets in the historical part are still very narrow, only about 1-meter wide, and vividly recall this Muslim past. Most of the squares and streets have kept their original names and refer to the fortified town: for example, Muro (Wall), Castillo (Castle), Fortaleza (Fort), or Puerta del Mar (Sea Gate). The Arabs remained for centuries until they capitulated in 1485 and handed the keys of the town to the Catholic conquerors.

Catholic reconquest

With the arrival of Los Reyes Católicos (Catholic Kings), everything changed with churches being built and roads being widened. To protect the town, five defense towers were added to the existing four. Eventually, the 34-meter high tower of the Iglesia de la Encarnación church would come to dominate the town. Then there is the charming Capilla de San Juan Dios church, set between Calle Caridad and Misericordia. It is often referred to as the 'Hospitalillo' because it was built by the Kings as a town hospital.

The Catholic Kings gave the Arabs or Hispano-Muslims three options. They could stay and convert to Christianity, leave

Marbella to live inland, or return to northern Africa. The Hispanic-Muslims who renounced their religion were called the 'moriscos' and the ones who kept it were the 'mudéjars'. But when the moriscos kept their traditions, the restrictions became more severe and unbearable, finally ending in the Morisco Revolt. This chapter of history is not one of the nicest as it ended in many lives being lost. It all came to an end with the edict to expel them from Spain in 1613.

Christianity is deeply rooted in Spanish life and remains relevant today. There are many little corners with hermitages and statues of María, starting at the port pier, in the villages, and on the forest trails. Here, people of all generations are deeply religious and have managed to keep traditions alive. There are many legends and stories to be told, and you'll find more of them in the descriptions of the hikes and villages.

Industrial revolution: 19th to 20th-century working class

Iron was discovered in the Sierra Blanca mountain in the early 19th century and was soon booming after providing lots of jobs. But when this industry slowed down and eventually closed, the workers returned to farming and fishing, with most of the population remaining poor.

The Spanish civil war didn't bring any relief either, when many buildings were burned down or seized by the Nationalists under the dictator Francisco Franco. This leader liked to entertain his friends here, including José Banús. After WWII, Marbella remained a working-class village with only about 900 inhabitants.

Jet-set

The tourism industry would soon change the region. When Alfonso Von Hohenlohe converted his family holiday resort into the legendary Marbella Club hotel in 1954 for his aristocratic circles, he had no idea of the long-term impact his actions would have on the economy, town, and region. The Puerto Banús and Puente Romano complexes followed later in the 1970s, as did endless other high-end developments. These included the residence—which looks like the American White House—of King Fahd of Saudi Arabia, who was a friend of Von Hohenlohe. The Saudi royal family has long had ties with Marbella, generating wealth in the area by buying land and building lots of properties. Their presence has also given rise to many extravagant stories, including bringing in a fleet of Mercedes cars from Germany for their private guests or hiring 15 orchestras from around the world for the King's granddaughter's wedding of more than 1000 guests.

PART 1.1. Marbella Coastal Paths: blue sea with history

Wooden footpaths along the coast of Málaga

Recent years have seen the ongoing addition of new wooden footpaths to Marbella´s beaches. They connect the existing promenades making your walking experience refreshingly new, fun, and interesting. Now, you can stroll for long distances over the 27-km coastline of Marbella and beyond. This is due to Marbella being included in an ambitious sustainable project called the Senda Litoral de Málaga (Coastal Path of Málaga). This extraordinary venture stretches over 180 km of coastline and connects the beaches of 14 coastal municipalities from Manilva to Nerja in Málaga province. Building this trail is an ambitious challenge because some stretches are difficult to link up: the land isn't always flat, and cliffs or other barriers stand in the way. Carefully designed bridges have been placed to overcome these problems, while also taking harsh sea conditions into account. They are made of sturdy wood with handrails, and completely blend in with the natural settings. Apart from creating local business opportunities, the project will make the coast more attractive for visitors, who will be able to enjoy the rich natural and cultural heritage of the area, walk near ancient ruins, or stop by sites with fascinating bird species. Information boards have also been placed along the Senda Litoral to increase awareness of the immense variety of coastal flora and fauna and their great ecological value.

This coastal project goes hand in hand with another large-scale plan, the Gran Senda de Málaga (Great Málaga Path), which is an 850-km circular walking trail that goes through the whole province of Málaga and runs over beautiful and wide-ranging landscapes. Some of the walks share stretches with the Málaga Coastal Path, such as stage 31, which begins on Marbella´s promenade and ends in Ojén.

Marbella's beaches have been designated as eco-reserves to raise awareness and make sure the dunes, flora, and fauna are respected. The recently placed information boards help walkers appreciate the richness of the area. Other changes are under way in Marbella: for example, the sustainable city model of the Marbella Strategic Plan-San Pedro 2022. This plan will create urban walks with information boards highlighting the rich biodiversity of the town.

Marbella and its surroundings are truly becoming a destination for all tastes. So who knows? Apart from the nickname "Costa del Golf" (Golf Coast), the Costa del Sol might become the "Costa del Senderismo" (Hiking Coast).

Open your eyes and walk through Marbella´s history

At the time of writing, you can stroll over walkways from Marbella´s Los Monteros beach to San Pedro de Alcántara, apart from a small stretch at Playa del Cable beach where you need to walk on the sand. Since this is a long-distance walk with many points of cultural interest, it has been divided into two medium-size routes; from Los Monteros to Puerto Banús and from Puerto Banús to San Pedro. We also suggest a third route connecting the boundary of Marbella at Cabopino to Mijas. This is a not-to-be-missed ecological coastline walk. Each of these routes is illustrated with a story, legend or bit of history to spice up your walk. Historic watchtowers, luxury hotels and residential complexes are found over the entire Marbella coastline. There are also four marinas, each with their own charm and characteristics. The town centres of San Pedro de Alcántara and Marbella are very different, despite being in the same municipality and sharing the white-village features typical of Andalusia. Both of them merit their own stories. For example, San Pedro has archaeological ruins and Marbella has a richer historical centre. Walk around and be open to whatever crosses your path. Whether impressive or discrete, big or small, all the works of art, architecture and landmarks have something to say and offer insights into a vibrant Marbella. So, let them speak to you and find out what made Marbella what it is today. Every point of interest is worth a book on its own: here I am only lifting a tiny corner of the veil.

WALK 1: DUNES AND WATCHTOWERS: CABOPINO TO MIJAS

The facts

Type:	Linear
Length:	10 km
Level:	Easy
Elevation gain:	23 m
Time:	2 h

What to expect

Can you imagine how Marbella and the coastline must have looked before tourism and intense construction kicked off in the 1960s, when dunes and historical towers dominated the landscape? Today, what remains of this natural and cultural heritage has been restored and protected for everybody to visit and enjoy.

The walk starts with a little stroll through the dunes at Cabopino beach, goes on to the yacht harbour, and then links up with the well-kept footpaths of Mijas. Just after the harbour, there is a short stretch over the sand.

However, most of this route is on wooden walkways that cross the sand dunes close to the waves. The beaches are narrow on this side and rocky areas host protected fauna and flora, offering wonderful spots for bird-watchers and photographers. At the start and finish of the walk, the mountains of the Sierra Blanca in Marbella and the Sierra de Mijas can be seen in the distance.

History, stories and more

Protection of the dunes

The dunes of Cabopino are located east of Marbella at Playa de Artola.

They are the result of a long natural process driven by powerful winds and waves that pushed the sand inland to form dunes.

There are three types: rippled dunes closest to the sea, then mobile dunes with plants such as marram grass and beautiful sea daffodils, and finally, further inland, fossil dunes with pine trees.

With construction for the tourism industry booming, the Junta de Andalucía declared an area of 192,715 m² as a Natural Monument in 2001 to avoid the complete loss of this natural enclave to further construction. Wooden footbridges now crisscross the dunes to protect them from damage and offer tourists a more enjoyable experience.

Coastal watchtowers from a turbulent past

There are no less than 42 watchtowers on the coast of Málaga province. Six of them are located within the area of Marbella. They are the remains of a line of fortification towers dating back to Moorish times, when the coastline had to be defended against invaders. The Catholic monarchs kept using this military system and many new towers were added over time to prevent attacks from pirates. Beacon fires were lit at the tops of the towers to warn others of approaching enemy ships. The smoke could be seen from the surrounding towers and the coastal defence would be alerted to come to their aid. At a later period, the towers had their own artillery. In 1985, the towers were declared sites of Cultural Interest.

Towers of the Thieves, Calahonda and Mijas

You'll come across three defence towers on this coastal walk. The 15-m high Torre de los Ladrones (Tower of the Thieves) is said to be the highest on the Málaga coastline. The materials used and its shape clearly show that it was built by the Arabs. The Torre Vigía de Calahonda or Calahorra (the Calahonda Watchtower) lies on private property along the walkway and is around 10-m high. It was built between the 16th and 18th centuries to reinforce the existing network of coastal watch-towers. This is also the case of the Torreón de la Cala de Mijas (the Tower of Mijas), which marks the end of the walk and has a visitor centre/museum.

The Torreón forms a half-circle and has two short spurs at the back. It was built in the 18th century and is entirely made of stone. Inside, there are two floors and a roof terrace, with the main room on the upper floor. This room was covered with brick vaulting and had a large chimney to produce warning smoke.

Cabopino marina

Hidden between pine trees and dunes is the cosy Puerto Deportivo (marina) of Cabopino. This is the last of four marinas built in Marbella in 1978. It has a very different character from the other marinas because it was designed for smaller leisure yachts and is tucked away from the busy crowds of central Marbella.

Driving directions

On the AP-7, take the Cabopino exit. The car park is on the right, just before you enter the harbour.

Step-by-step walking guide

- Once parked, have a stroll through the dunes on the wooden footpath turning right. When you reach the Torre de Ladrones, turn left onto the beach and walk a few metres on the sand.

- Pass by the Cabopino marina and walk again for about half a kilometre on the sand.

- You'll get to a paved footpath at Playa Calahonda that leads to the Mijas coastal area. On the way, you will see some residential buildings.

- You soon arrive at the spectacular coastal wooden bridges. From here, you can see a huge range of birds or even sometimes spot whales, as described on the information boards.

- The walk curves around a private property, where you can see the Calahonda tower, and continues along Calahorra beach.

- Cross the Calahorra river and continue on the paved footpath to la Cala de Mijas square, where you can see its tower.

Walk 2: From old Marbella to jet-set Marbella. Los Monteros, the centre & the Golden Mile walk

The facts

Type:	Linear-one way
Length:	14 km
Level:	Easy
Time:	2.5 h

What to expect

Monuments, landmarks, art and architecture will tell you the story of Marbella while you enjoy a walk by the sea on the new and old beach promenades. A small detour into the old town is a must to fully appreciate the rich cultural heritage at hand and connect the old town with the new Marbella. For centuries, this stretch must have looked like a defensive wall on an endless beach with the mountains behind. Marbella stayed a small fishing village for a long time and it was only about 60 years ago that it became an international all-year-round luxury resort attracting millions of visitors each year.

This route is very straightforward: it's simply a walk along the promenade from the east to the west of Marbella with a small detour into the old town. The different areas of the town and the promenade have their own stories, legends and histories. This walk highlights and connects some of them, so you can walk by the sea while enjoying these cultural attractions.

History, stories and more

Los Monteros

The emblematic Los Monteros hotel, one of the first five star hotels in Marbella, dates back to 1962. The hotel's La Cabane beachclub formula was a pioneer in its time on the Costa del Sol and the restaurant of the hotel was the first to receive a

Michelin star in Spain. Since then, the area around the hotel has been developed with high-end properties and is still a prime location in Marbella, along with many others.

Torre del Mineral & Virgen del Carmen

The strange concrete tower in the sea is also a symbol that harks back to the industrial era of Marbella in the mid-20th century. Today, it has become a landmark monument called the Torre del Mineral or Torre del Cable. It served as part of a funicular system with a monocable that transported minerals from the mines in the nearby mountains of Ojén to the cargo ships anchored offshore as these could not enter the Bajadilla marina.

Sailors and fishermen are protected by their Patron Saint of the Sea, the Virgen del Carmen, whose statue lies under the sea all year round. But once a year, on the 16th of July, divers bring her to the surface and take her by boat for the nautical and land-based processions. The Virgin is carried around Marbella among deeply moved locals and amazed tourists until reaching her destination at the Encarnación church. Once the processions are over, the statue of the virgin is returned to the bottom of the sea for another year. When life is hard, belief gives hope. Nobody can tell the story of hardship in Marbella better than its own people. A lively old local woman recounted the tale of the harsh life she led as a typical fisherman's wife. Every day, her husband would leave their tiny house to fish in the seas at around 5 a.m., regardless of the sea conditions. She would then wait anxiously until the appointed woman would knock on her door to announce the safe arrival of her husband.

Marbella´s two central marinas

On this walk you'll see the Puertos deportivos (sports marinas) of Bajadilla and Virgen del Carmen. They are near each other and connected by the beach promenade. The Puerto deportivo de Bajadilla is beautiful and well-kept, although its location is a little unfortunate, as it is next to an industrial area and the Quirón hospital. It dates from 1961 and used to be the fishermen's marina until it was modernized in 2000 to better accommodate leisure boats. The Puerto deportivo Virgen del Carmen is right in the heart of the town, only a stroll away from the Avenida del Mar and the historical centre. Both visitors and locals flock to the port as a centre of activity. It's near to popular beaches and is filled with bars, restaurants and water-sports clubs for visitors to enjoy.

Open-air museum

Ten bronze sculptures by the eccentric Salvador Dalí decorate the marble boulevard Avenida del Mar that connects the sea promenade with the centre. They are copies made from smaller originals. The stairs lead to the Alameda park with a large round fountain dating from the 18th century, which is dedicated to the Virgen del Rocio. The park is a refreshing green oasis where the community can meet and chat on benches made of Andalusian tiles and decorated with drawings of Marbella and surroundings.

The Casco Antiguo (Old Town)

A pleasant stroll takes you through the maze of narrow winding cobbled streets of the old town referred to as the Casco antiguo of Marbella. It's full of shops, tapa´s bars, squares, chapels and churches and dozens of little secret corners. Little remains of the town's Roman origins: among these are the 3 Ionic capitals embedded in the Moorish castle walls. The Arabs left the largest mark when they fortified the town with a strong wall and a castle, the Alcazaba, under Abd Al Rahman III in the 10th century. Positioned on a hill about 30 meters above sea level, the towers of the castle allowed good visual military control of the area. The centre, or Medina, was later destroyed and replaced by the Catholic Monarchs with the Plaza de los Naranjos. They built some churches, including the 15th-century Santiago hermitage and several public buildings, and converted Marbella into an economic, administrative and social centre for the entire region. In the 19th century, houses were built in the interior of the castle and only the walls were left.

Today, colourful flowers and rows of orange trees decorate the Plaza de los Naranjos. It is surrounded by historic whitewashed buildings, such as the Mudejar-style Mayor's house dating from the 16th century. In the centre of the square, squeezed between the patio tables serving typical Andalusian dishes, there is a bronze bust of the previous Spanish King Juan Carlos. Not far away, there's the grandiose Iglesia de Nuestra Señora de la Encarnación (Church of Our Lady of the Incarnation), which was founded in 1618 as a second version of the church that had already replaced an old mosque. The church is under the protective eye of St. Bernard, the patron saint of Marbella, whose statue stands in the beautiful square with its cross-shaped fountain.

El Faro

El Faro (the lighthouse) was built in 1864 and measures 29 metres. Every 14.5 seconds it automatically emits two bright flashes which are visible 41-km away.

The Golden Mile

The Golden Mile starts at the copper tower on the Plaza Bocanegra (near Cappuccino bar on the promenade) and defines the luxurious residential and high-end tourism area between Marbella centre and Puerto Banus. Mid-way the very elegant beach promenade, is the legendary Marbella Club Hotel. Marbella changed forever when Prince Alfonso von Hohenlohe converted his parents´ finca into the Marbella Club Hotel which opened its doors in 1954. Alfonso and Ricardo Soriano, the 2nd Marquis of Ivanrey who built el Rodeo a few years earlier, were pioneers in making Marbella known internationally. They had an excellent network of aristocratic friends, royalty and celebrities and invited them to Marbella. Many followed in their footsteps and invested in the area. Following the success of the hotel, Alfonso launched later the idea of building the most exclusive Puente Romano apartment complex and hotel. Both hotels have kept their legendary status and you pass them on the promenade by the wooden pier. The entire area around is flanked with high-end properties, shops and restaurants, which is why it was named the Golden Mile of Marbella.

Roman ruins

The Puente Romano hotel was named after a 1st-century Roman bridge found in the area. The bridge formed a tiny part of the long Via Augusta Roman road that connected Cadiz with Rome. The charming cobblestone bridge, which has been extensively renovated, is beautifully located in the midst of the hotel's courtyard and gardens. You have to go into the hotel's courtyard to see it. It's a very romantic spot to take photos.

Pop around the corner just before crossing the Rio Verde to have a look at a tiny but rather special Roman villa ruin from the 1st century that belonged to the Roman city of Cilniana. Unique to this site is the floor with its white and black mosaic tiles depicting very unusual images of clothing, kitchen utensils, meat dishes and fish food, which reveal a little more about life in Roman days. The image of Medusa's head with its snakes is typical as it was a Roman custom to use it to scare away possible intruders. Strangely enough, the one depicted here is a friendlier and maybe more decorative version.

Driving directions

On the AP-7 going toward Málaga, take the first exit just after Rio Torre Real towards Reserva Los Monteros. Keep going until the end of the road and turn left to the beach, where there is a small car park.

Step-by-step walking guide

- Turn right at the end of the wooden footpath on Playa Realejo that runs over the beautiful eco-reserve of dunes. The path passes the Rio Real (Royal River), which rises in the mountain-village of Ojén, then next to a golf course until it ends on the Playa del Pinillo beach with its chiringuito.

- Walk alongside the chiringuito and re-connect with the 2 km of wooden footbridges running over a pebble beach and dunes again, and approach the town centre at the Playa del Cable.

- Walk on the pathway for about 600 m to the Bajadilla marina.

- Walk through the marina and fishermen's quarters

with their intense blue doors on white facades evoking the times of traditional wooden boats.

- Connect with the paved promenade in central Marbella at Playa de la Bajadilla. Further on, you'll pass Playa Venus, where there is the landmark Hotel Fuerte. This was the first hotel opened in central Marbella in 1957. Take a peep through the hotel gate to see the remains of the fort built during the reign of Carlos V in 1554 as a defence against pirates.

Historic Centre – short detour:

- Walk up the stairs of the Avenida del Mar with its marble promenade and Dalí statues and the next stairs to the Alameda park. Cross the road and enter the old town via the cobbled street.

- At the small square with some bar terraces, where they serve very typical Spanish churros (long thin doughnuts), take a right turn into the Alameda alley and then straight to the beautiful San Juan de Dios chapel (16th century).

- Go left from the chapel towards the Incarnation church, and get your first glimpse of the castle wall.

- Walk into Trinidad street next to the castle wall to the Plaza Sepulcro.

- Follow the wall left into Salinas street and then take the stairs to stroll around the beautiful pond in the exotic Arroyo de la Represa park, which is mainly used by the locals.

- Go back to the castle wall and into Portada street.

- Go left into Escuela street and then to Plaza de San Barnabé. If you turn right you'll reach the Plaza de los Naranjos.

- At the Ermita de Santiago (Chapel of Santiago), take the small street that goes back down to the Alameda park and the beach promenade.

Beach promenade continued:

- Walk past the Virgen del Carmen marina and the Fontanilla beach, pass the tourism centre, the statue of the waterskiing woman, and later on the Faro lighthouse.

- Cross the stream coming from the mountains. This roughly marks the start of the Golden mile.

- The paved promenade changes into a sandy promenade at the Pesquera restaurant and Casablanca beach.

- At the playa de Nagueles are the Puente Romano hotel and Marbella club hotel with its stone and wooden pier.

- At Victor´s beach look out for the watchtower El Alcón on the hill on your right.

- A little behind the Besaya beach restaurant you'll find the Museo Ralli (Ralli Museum). This museum hosts contemporary Latin American and European art and includes works by Dalí and Miró.

- The walk ends at the red wooden bridge. It was built over the Rio Verde in 2010 to connect the promenades of Puerto Banús with the Golden Mile. Just before the bridge, in the Calle Carlos Posac Mon street parallel to the beach promenade, you can find the Roman site of Rio Verde.

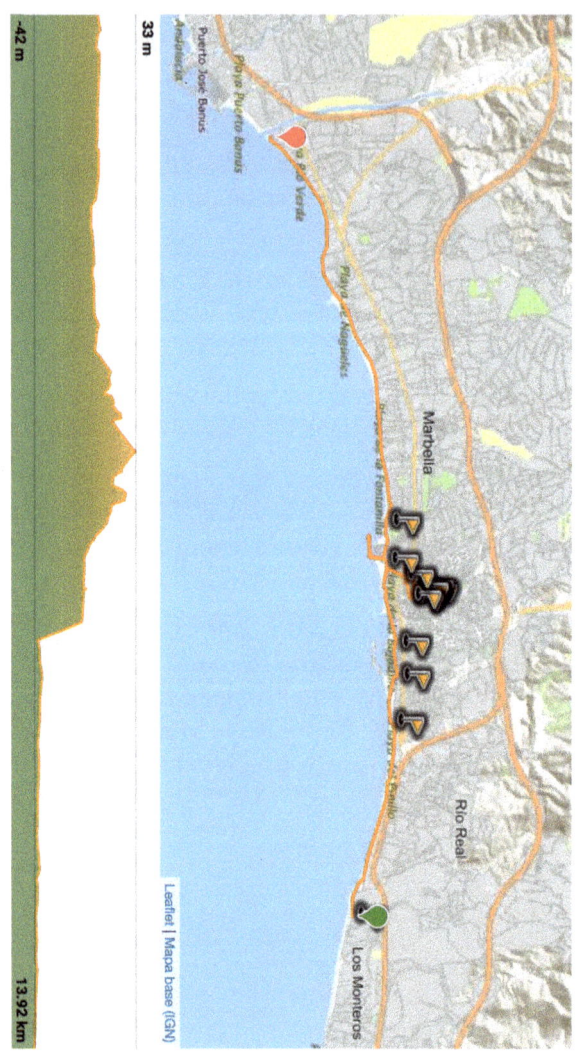

WALK 3: PUERTO BANÚS TO SAN PEDRO: WOODEN BRIDGES AND ARCHAEOLOGICAL SITES

The facts

Type:	Partly linear, partly circular
Length:	10.5 kilometres
Level:	Easy
Elevation gain:	34 meters
Time:	2.5 hours

What to expect

Walk from the glamorous Puerto Banús marina along the sea-front into the authentic white-village centre of San Pedro with its contrasting new boulevards in this rapidly changing part of town. You'll discover hidden corners that you might easily overlook on an ordinary beach walk. Imagine the different feelings and sensations the seaside would have awoken in people over time: how did it feel hundreds or even thousands of years ago? You can get a taste by focusing on the buildings and architecture. As a place for well-being: the Roman baths; as a reminder of the constant threat from invaders: the watchtowers; as an inspiration for modern design: the boulevard bridge; and today as a place to relax. Contemplate these echoes of the past during your walk: these archaeological sites have stood the test of time and bear witness to its history.

After making your way past the chic boutiques and impressive yachts of Puerto Banús, your walk runs over the beach on well-kept walkways and wooden paths. A little inland detour will take you to the small archaeological sites of Las Bóvedas and Vega del Mar in the older residential areas of San Pedro. Then it goes in the direction of the old town through the newer part of San Pedro with its wide avenues, immaculate gardens, large fountains and designer bridge.

History, stories and more

The Puerto Banús project

The luxurious Puerto Banús marina, developed by José Banús, was meant to have its own jet-set identity right from the start. The inauguration party in 1970 was attended by aristocracy, celebrities and royalty including Prince Rainier of Monaco and Grace Kelly. The marina could accommodate super-yachts and provided high-end shopping for the most demanding clients in an architectural setting resembling a cosy white Andalusian village. It was the pearl in the crown of a larger project west of Marbella: Nueva Andalucia. José Banús wanted to appeal to a rich international clientele at a time when Marbella was an exclusive destination mainly for aristocratic families from Europe. Ever since then, its success has continued to grow with the addition of many more high-end shops, restaurants and hotels. Apart from the wealthy and famous who visit or moor their super-yachts here, it also attracts around five million visitors each year.

Art and the tower at Puerto Banús

The entrance to Puerto Banús has two roundabouts with sculptures. The first one, at Cristamar, is a rhinoceros by the master of surrealism, the Spanish artist Salvador Dalí. Full of typical Dalí sexual symbols, the rhino´s horn refers to sex, the lace to femininity, and the sea-urchins to power. The statue weighs three tons and was made in 1956 following his movie "The Prodigious Adventure of the Lacemaker and the

Rhinoceros". On the second roundabout, closer to the sea, is a 26-m granite column topped with a bust of José Banús. This was made by the Georgian monumental artist, Zurab Tsereteli, and was a gift from the Mayor of Moscow to Puerto Banús.

Despite being 11-m high, you could easily miss the somewhat hidden Torre del Duque, a completely restored watchtower built between the 13th and 15th century. You can find it in the gardens of Gray d´Albion, a private beachside residential complex at the exit of the Puerto Banús marina. The tower is named after the Duke of Cádiz and Arcos, Rodrigo Ponce de Léon, who was one of the main captains under the Catholic monarchs during the conquest of Granada. The Duke loved to restore historical buildings.

San Pedro´s Roman bath, Tower & Basilica

The 2nd-century Roman thermae and the 16th-century watchtower are right next to each other, although there's more than a

thousand years between them. Both are on the archaeological site of Las Bóvedas by Guadalmina beach.

Little is known about them as historical sources are scarce, but the thermae has a clear polygonal design with several rooms around it for hot, mild and cold bathing. Roman construction ingenuity made the vaulted ceiling so strong that it is still partly preserved today.

The tower was built by the Christian rulers only a few meters from the baths. It's conical, 13-m high, and 8.20 meters in diameter at the base. What remains uncertain is whether the Christian rulers used the baths to store weapons or as another defence emplacement.

A little further inland is the 6th-century Visigothic basilica Vega de Mar, which was built on top of a 3rd-century Roman necropolis. Only the 1-m-high walls of the basilica remain. The plan has three naves and two opposed semi-circular apses. The well-preserved baptismal font is to be said the only one of its kind in Europe and it gives a glimpse into the ritual of converting people from the World of Darkness into the Kingdom of God. The entire body had to be immersed three times—in the name of the Father, the Son, and the Holy Spirit—and then the newborn clean Christian was allowed to enter the sacred temple.

Dizzy sea-waves bridge on the boulevard

The new bridge was designed to evoke the feeling of the sea. Its shape mimics sea waves and on the highest point you can see the sea and San Pedro beach promenade. It also reflects the spirit behind the project as it had to be fun for families, have a community feel and be a place for social gathering. This 54000-m² urban park project, called the `bulevar´, gave a very welcome economic, social and aesthetic boost to San Pedro village, which previously was split into two parts by the busy national Mediterranean road. This project marked the beginning of the modernisation of San Pedro, bringing it into the 21st century.

San Pedro old town

San Pedro lies on a wide coastal plain surrounded by hills. It was founded in 1861 by the first Marquis del Duero, Manuel Gutiérrez de la Concha y Irigoyen as a farming colony for the emergent sugar cane industry. The village has tiny white houses grouped around a modernised square with a parish

church. The original church was burned down during the Civil War in 1936, but restored 7 years later. The old town is now connected to the new boulevard by the Marques del Duero avenue. In the distance, one can see the mountains of Sierra del Real (north), Sierra de las Nieves and Sierra Blanca (east), and Monte Mayor and Sierra Bermeja (west).

Driving directions

Enter Puerto Banús at the first exit after the Nagüeles tunnel as you come from Marbella or Málaga. At the rhino roundabout, turn left into the long Calle los Granados street, where there is a free car park at the red wooden bridge.

Step-by-step walking guide

- Start at the red wooden bridge that crosses the Rio Verde in Puerto Banús.

- Keep walking along the paved walkway by the sea-front until the end, at `la Sirena´ (a statue of a white mermaid by Antonio Cañete) and the round-about with a column and bronze sculpture.

- Turn left into the marina with super-yacht moorings.

To get the best views of Puerto Banús, take a stroll on the pier before continuing.

- The promenade continues at the harbour's sea entrance behind the Torre del Duque watchtower, and then goes along the beach on a wooden walkway until reaching the Ocean Beach club. Go up the stairs on the promenade and have a look at the sculpture of Lola Flores. She was an icon of Andalusian dancing and singing and in 1962 bought a house in Marbella that she named `Los Gitanillos´.

- There are several stone piers at Playa Nueva Andalucia.

- The path narrows between the Guadalpin Banus hotel terrace and the beach, but continues on the rocky beach towards San Pedro. After about 1 km, the path makes a little detour inland to cross the river Guadaiza. It then connects with the wide paved San Pedro promenade, which you walk on until the end.

- Leave the promenade and continue on the beach through the trees between the local fishermen's boats and storage huts until the Avenida Carmen Sevilla road. On the right there is the archaeological basilica site, but first we make a small detour on the left towards the beach and the Las Bóvedas site. To get there, turn left on the Avenida Carmen Sevilla.

- At the jet ski centre walk on the beach, cross the Chopo river, and pass the Macao beach restaurant.

- After a few meters you can see the Las Bóvedas monuments.

- Make your way back to the Avenida Carmen Sevilla and turn right into the Calle los Eucaliptos, where you'll find the entrance to the Palaeochristian basilica of Vega de Mar.

- Continue on this road leading through an older area of San Pedro with many one-floor houses.

- At the end turn left into the wide road, which is divided by a central strip with a pleasant footpath that leads toward the boulevard and village of San Pedro.

- At the far end there is a blue and white boat. Cross over the large roundabout and walk straight ahead on the attractive wide avenue of Marques del Duero. Then, stroll through the narrow streets until you reach the centre of San Pedro at the Plaza de la Iglesia with its beautiful parish church. Afterward, make your way back to the boulevard.

- Walk over the wooden wave-shaped bridge towards Marbella where you can see the Sierra Blanca mountain in the distance.

- At the roundabout, go right on the Avenida de la Coruña, and head toward the sea.

- Turn into the first street on the left (Calle Guadaiza) and past the green.

- Cross the road and take the first street on the right to the roundabout.

- At the roundabout, turn right into the wider Avenida Petunias street, leading towards the sea and the tall ballet dancer sculpture. At this point, turn left and you will be on the same path you came from.

- If you like, you can make a short detour at the river. Cross the road bridge onto the footpath Paseo Fluvial Ramón that runs inland parallel with the river. After the tunnel, there's a large unfenced meadow on the right where bulls are happily grazing.

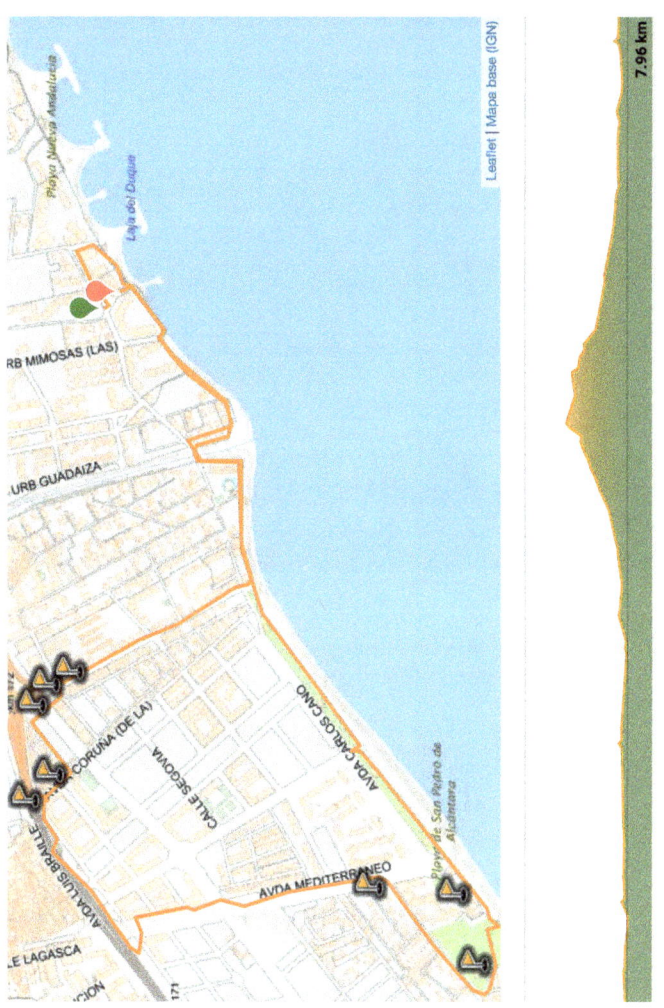

Part 1.2. Marbella Mountain Paths: the Sierra Blanca Nature Reserve

It's almost impossible not to fall in love with the unique landscape of Marbella's endless hills, blue sea and its emblematic landmark, the 'Sierra Blanca' mountains.

Marbella lies right at the foothills of this marvellous mountain range with their steep slopes rising to an altitude of 1,275 metres. The mountain range hugs Marbella like a protective coat ensuring a year round mild micro-climate with much-loved average temperatures of 18°C.

In scientific terms, the Sierra Blanca is part of the southern Penibaetic mountain ranges that run from Murcia to Cádiz. The Sierra spreads over 6500 ha and nestles between the coastline of Marbella and the more inland Sierra de las Nieves national park. It's bordered by the municipalities of Istán and Ojén on either side and Monda in the north. Sierra Blanca means 'White Mountain' and refers to the scarce vegetation on the upper slopes leaving the pale grey limestone rock exposed. This greyish colour makes for an interesting contrast with the neighbouring red-coloured Sierra Bermeja mountain, which is also visible from Marbella looking towards Estepona.

The mountain is rich in water with several mountain springs and streams, so crossing some on your walks is not rare. The most typical ones are the Arroyo de Molinos (Istán), Arroyo de los Monjes (Xarblanca), Arroyo de las Piedras (Camoján) and the two main rivers on its perimeter, the Rio Verde and the Rio Real, that flow into the sea at Marbella. The Sierra Blanca mountain range is one of the closest to the sea and has several tall peaks. The most widely known is 'La Concha' that stands at 1,215 metres and was named after the shell-like shape of the peak. The intense climb to this peak is a favourite of many passionate hikers. However, the less well-known 'Pico del Lastonar' wins the altitude prize at close to 1,275 metres. The most frequently visited peak is the 'Cruz de Juanar' at 1,184 metres, as this easy hike is accessible to hikers of all levels including children.

Fauna and flora

On your walk, you'll see a diverse array of trees, plants, and colourful flowers including the most flamboyant orchids. These flowers are protected here as they are slowly becoming extinct. Trees rule the mountain and cover 94% of it. Most of the forest comprises groups of scattered trees, while the rest is formed of dense trees, impenetrable shrubs, and rocks. To name just a few, there are cork oaks, wild olive trees, pines, chestnut, and eucalyptus trees. Pines are almost sacred in the entire region and removing them even in your own back yard is not allowed. The Aleppo pine is a widely used tree for forest regeneration on the mountain.

When you are out on the walks, don't forget you are entering the territory of a wide range of animals. These include various types of smaller reptiles, such as salamanders and lizards, but there are also small- to medium-sized snakes. Of these, the viper *Vipera Latastei* is poisonous. There's also a huge number of wild boars. Luckily, you won't often see them as they tend to avoid places where humans go. However, there are species we do like to see, including small colourful birds such as the striped Hoopoe, as well as impressive eagles, falcons, and other raptors. Every year a group of storks stop here on their long migration to and from Africa and on a lucky day, you might see them fly over. But there can be only one king of the region and that is the mountain goat. These animals often show up rather unexpectedly as they cross the mountain roads in herds. Their cute heads can also be spotted on the higher sunny rocks at the Mirador de Montés viewpoint.

At last: protected status

Until recently, the Sierra Blanca was not protected as a natural park or reserve of any kind. Luckily, this has started to change and since 2015 it has proudly formed part of the Red Natura 2000, an ambitious initiative by the European Union to conserve biodiversity, species, habitats, and spaces and protect the ecosystems we need so badly. This initiative is important for migrating birds that use the Sierra Blanca as a safe green passage. Hopefully, the Sierra Blanca will soon be protected as part of the Sierra de las Nieves National Park, which surrounds it.

A little dive into the past... when the mountain was part of daily life

Although the mountain used to be a very important part of daily life, these days it has become a natural heritage as well as a paradise for sportspeople. Not that long ago, the narrow footpaths, of which some 89.7 kilometres are officially recognised, were of fundamental importance to the villagers, muleteers, shepherds, farmers, and fishermen, who would hike up the mountain to reach the nearby villages and collect natural ingredients or deliver their products. Puerto Rico (behind La Cañada) used to be an agricultural centre, which explains the surprising amount of planted fruit and olive trees between the wilder vegetation. Miners were also at work to exploit the mountains' rich mineral resources, such as zinc, iron, nickel, and lead. And then there were the monks ('monjes'), who would seek solitude for prayer and meditation, considering the surrounding nature and its rivers as holy. There were no hospitals, roads, and facilities as we know them now, but there was religion. This explains the little hermitages and Maria sculptures that are in every corner, starting at the port peer, in the villages, and on the forest trails. Of course, there are endless stories to be told, and you'll find more of them in the description of the hike and villages.

Walking trails

Over time, the trails fell out of use and became overgrown and inaccessible. In the last decade, private and public initiatives helped to open them up so people could enjoy hiking, a form of tourism that has massively expanded in recent years. The mountain now has an excellent network of trails, and more of these are gradually being recognized and officially mapped. Most are in good condition and well signposted with the names of places or directions.

Paths have varying levels of difficulty, and range from easy to very hard depending on the elevation gain or how much care you have to take. This information is never indicated on the signposts. Most trails are easily accessible, but some are narrow and rocky and sometimes run over steep slopes with pronounced elevation gains or losses. They can be trickier to follow and it is not uncommon for someone to get lost or walk for far longer than anticipated as many trails cross each other. So be prepared to read the signposts and where they lead to or download your map. There is a mix of old wooden signposts with many named 'puerto', which means mountain pass. There are also newer information panels and signposts which also indicate the remaining distance to the destination. These include those on the Gran Senda de Malaga, the 850-kilometre circular route that runs through Málaga Province and passes through Marbella.

The walks that begin up on the mountain mostly start from the lodge called the Refugio de Juanar before the entrance of the park. There is plenty of parking space around it and also on the way up to the gates of the park itself. This is the spot where families gather on the weekends to have a short walk up to the panoramic viewpoints or collect chestnuts in autumn.

Whichever walk you choose, with good preparation, you'll enjoy this fantastic natural heritage and be wowed by the simply spectacular landscape and views of the Mediterranean Sea, the African coast, the Strait of Gibraltar, and all the surrounding mountain region in the area.

Important information

You can do the walks all year round, but they are especially enjoyable in spring when there is a display of coloured flowers and the temperature is mild. In the hot summer months, a very early rise is recommended, but avoid the walk if there is a risk of forest fires. On winter days, it can be surprisingly cold so wear layers of clothing (even gloves at times!). After heavy rain, the trails can get muddy and slippery.

Don't forget: your best friends are decent hiking shoes, walking sticks and, most importantly, lots of water and sun protection.

And make sure your friends and family are equally well prepared, as it goes without saying, if one suffers, the whole group does.

Starting points and driving directions

From the Marbella area, you can access the mountain from a range of starting points. Some are well-hidden unofficial trails. Up to a few years ago, hiking the mountain was a bit of an exploration, where map-reading skills came in handy and a strong sense of adventure even more. Since then, more signposts have been set up, but trails often cross and at times the names can still be confusing (or just missing). To try make life simple and hiking accessible for the worst of map readers, we've narrowed down the starting points to the four most well-known and accessible ones in the following areas: Nagüeles, Don Miguel (Trapiche), Puerto Rico (La Cañada shopping centre), and Juanar (up on the mountain). These walks are grouped according to their starting points and detailed driving directions are provided for each of them.

STARTING POINT NAGUELES

Driving directions

- On the AP-7, take the Nagüeles exit and follow the signpost for Swans senior school and Cantera Nagüeles (Starlite festival auditorium).

- **Starting Point, Nagueles Park:** At the end of the road from Swans school (Calle Lago de los Cisnes), you'll find the starting point for walks to the Sierra Blanca and the Cascada residential area. These are connected to the trails of the La Mantua/Puerto Rico area if you are looking for longer hikes.

- **Starting Point, Old road to Istán**: At the end of the road from Swans school (Calle Lago de los Cisnes), turn left, passing the Starlite auditorium entrance, and drive along the mountain until the road ends. The mountain trail towards Istán starts here.

WALK 4: THE OLD MINING FOREST TRAIL OF BUENAVISTA

The facts

Type:	Linear
Length:	5.4 kilometres <u>return</u>
Level:	Moderate
Elevation gain:	370 metres
Time:	2.5 hours <u>return</u>

What to expect

The walk takes you through the forest, where you can catch a glimpse of the shell-shaped Sierra Blanca mountain top. The route follows a well-defined mountain trail and strongly climbs in an almost straight line northwards alongside the mountain flank of the 'Cañada de las minas', offering great sea views of central Marbella. As it climbs, it runs between a wider gorge of beautiful grey cliffs and ends in a river of rocks, named 'Arroyo de las Piedras'. This river almost never has water except after prolonged periods of heavy rain. Higher up, there are some sections where the trail gives out and you'll walk on fairly big rocks.

In general, the walk is appropriate for all levels and ages and families will enjoy its educational aspects.

History, stories and more

Old mines

There are small old mines on this part of the mountain, although they are almost invisible as they are overgrown, forgotten, and difficult to access (which is good, because entering them is dangerous). The mining industry in the mountain area was booming in the 19th century and many families lived on this very hard labour. Lead used to be extracted from the rich soil and was sold to other mines under the name of 'Buenavista'. For commercial purposes, they built a structure to treat the mineral, including an oven to melt it and a water basin to wash it. These are the most visible remains of a very different but not-so-distant past. The mining activity lasted here for about 130 years until the 1960s.

Step-by-step walking guide

- Starting point: The entry to the forest begins at the end of the road up from Swans senior school. Enter the forest and walk up the trail. There are several small starting points here, even one with an official map, but all the trails lead to the same path going up the mountain.

- Follow the signposts of the GR249 on an almost 2-meter wide trail going up.

- The trail becomes narrower running alongside the mountain flank on your left and a valley full of pines, with the Arroyo de las Piedras further down on your right. Continue straight up following "Buenavista", while ignoring now the GR249 (which bends off right towards Ojén).

- A little up from the archaeological site, the trail turns sharp left next to the river and leads over big rocks.

- You now have to watch your feet a bit, but the trail is still fairly easy although rocky, passing a small white pilgrims' cross and zigzagging up the mountain: this is the end of this walk. Some like to adventure and continue their way up on the dried-up river of rocks. WARNING! If you want to hike in the direction La Concha, you must have a professional guide with you because the walk becomes dangerous. So, we'll stick to the fun and safe part of the itinerary and return.

- Make your way down over the same trail and enjoy rewarding views towards the sea and the Marbella coastline.

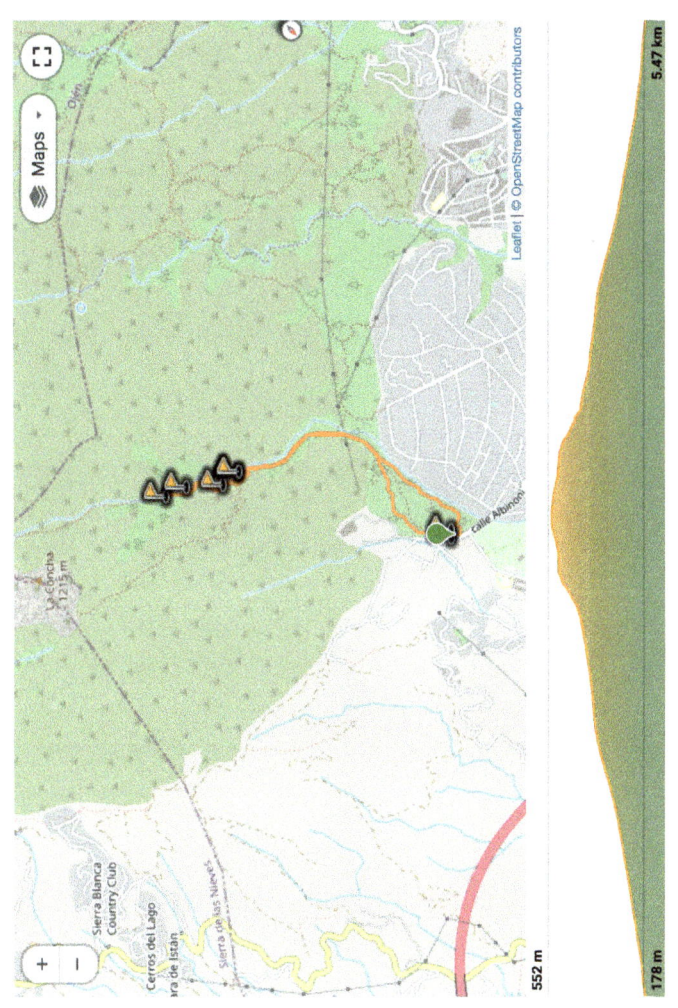

WALK 5: STUNNING LAKE VIEW WALK FROM MARBELLA TO ISTÁN VILLAGE

The facts

Type:	Linear (leave a car at Istán for your return!)
Length:	8.8 kilometres one-way
Level:	Moderate
Elevation:	353 metres
Time:	2.5-3 hours one-way

What to expect

Discover the west side of the Sierra Blanca mountain by the Istán lake. You can see it in the distance on many parts of this beautiful walk that mainly runs over narrow mountain trails. The walk is known as the 'Camino Viejo de Istán' or the 'old road to Istán': later, a tarmac road was built to connect Marbella with this lovely white village.

The first part of the walk is on a wide unpaved dirt road curving around the mountain slope on your right and along the valley on your left, where you are treated with views towards Puerto Banús. This part of the dirt road can get busy with walkers and mountain bikers, especially in the mornings after school drop-off when mums take the dogs out, so watch your step! There are also climbing clubs scaling the stunning grey cliff. The further you walk the quieter and more beautiful it gets as the spectacular Istán lake soon comes into view. After an initial but very short steep climb, you can enter the paved viewpoint on your right. This is worth a break because the views of the serene lake and the surrounding Sierra Bermeja mountains are simply breathtaking. After the climbers' cliff, the walk leaves the dirt road and turns onto a narrow steep mountain trail between scrubland. This is the part where longer trousers come in handy. From here, you gradually walk up mostly mountain trails which lead to an old tarmac road closer to the village. Overall, the trail is gentle, well maintained, and signposted.

The walk ends at the higher end of Istán at the refurbished Los Altos hotel with its heavenly location at the gateway of the Sierra de las Nieves national park and the grey peak named 'El Picacho', which is part of the Sierra Blanca mountain. But there isn't a better end to this walk than at a terrace bar on the apparently peaceful church square. In no time, you realize that this is actually a passage for the locals, who cut through the terraces and square in their cars to disappear into the narrow streets, leaving you behind with a little less healthy air….but still delicious tapas!

History, stories and more

Water source of the coast

The lake of Istán is actually a key water reservoir called the 'Pantano de la Concepción', into which the Rio Verde river flows ending in Puerto Banús. In 1971, a dam was built to address the critical water supply problems on the western side of the Costa del Sol. Today, at all times, the water level is carefully monitored. The alarm is raised if it's too low, or, more rarely, the precious water is unfortunately released into the sea if the dam has reached its capacity after a series of heavy rains.

Auditorio Nagüeles and Starlite

From far away, you can see the white letters of 'Auditorio Marbella' shine on the Sierra Blanca mountain. Every year, the Starlite music festival is celebrated in what was once the old Nagüeles quarry. The rocks were extracted in the late 1960s to build the new marina designed by José Banús. In 1983, Alfonso Hohenlohe, Julio Iglesias, and Plácido Domingo were the first artists to use the quarry creatively as an exceptional open-air natural auditorium. The venue was later abandoned for nearly 30 years, although the idea was fabulous. In 2012, the auditorium was finally restored into an impressive venue with ample seating, a stage in front of sand-coloured rock walls, and ready to host the summer Starlite festival. The event has been enormously successful, growing each year to become one of the leading music events in Spain, attracting famous international rock stars including Enrique Iglesias, Elton John, Lenny Kravitz, Lionel Richie, Andrea Bocelli, Ricky Martin, Tom Jones, and many others.

Important information

Don't forget that hiking in summer can be extremely hot, but, with an early rise, this side of the mountain provides you with a fair bit of shade. It really doesn't take long to drive two cars up to Istán, leave one behind, drive back down, and then set off. But if you do decide to return by bus to Marbella, check the timetable as there are only 3 bus rides per day (at the time of writing the bus hours are 07.45; 9.15; 16.00). You can always choose to walk back, but meanwhile, take your time to discover this pretty village or walk up to the viewpoint of the reservoir at the end of the village.

Driving directions to Istán to leave a car:

On the AP-7, coming from the direction of Marbella, take the A-7176 just after the tunnel. At the roundabout turn right and then left at the following roundabout. The road to Istán starts here next to the Manolo Santana tennis club. It is 12-kilometres or about a 20-minute drive up to the centre of Istán, where there is a parking area on your immediate right at the entrance to the village. Now drive back to the start of the walk at Nagüeles, as indicated above. It's a little bit of hassle before starting off on your hike, but for some it's a relief once reaching the village on foot.

Step-by-step walking guide

- Make your way to the Nagüeles starting point, along from Swans senior school. Take a left turn, passing the Starlite auditorium, until the road ends. You could walk this part, but we opt to drive and leave the car.

- Walk on the road, which is now unpaved and can get muddy after rain. After the first upwards slope, the road flattens and then gradually goes up while curving around the mountain. At a steeper part that angles right, you'll encounter a fantastic panoramic paved terrace on the right, 'Cantera la Legua', where you can rest and soak in the first spectacular views of the lake of Istán. This is the point where the municipality of

Marbella ends and Istán starts.

- Continue on the same unpaved road, which flattens out more beside the impressive vertical beige rock cliffs of Sierra Blanca.

- After about 2 kilometres, you have to leave the road via a mountain trail between scrubland: there's a signpost, but it's small, so watch out for it. Now the trail is straightforward to follow and, overall, gradually goes up. Occasionally, you may bump into one of the enthusiastic volunteers who maintain the footpath and cut the bushes that overgrow it.

- Once you reach the asphalted road at the abandoned residential area, turn right.

- After the building, take a right turn up an old tarmac road. This leads you back onto a mountain trail where you can follow the old PR140 signpost.

- Continue your walk and later on take a right turn again onto a wide old road. Keep going up the forest trail until you come to a stop with a deep canyon overgrown with bushes.

- Go left here, where the trail is narrow and a bit steep. You'll see the stunning reddish cliff of Tajo Bermejo on your way. Follow the trail until you reach the official road to Istán, where there is a signpost. There's only another 2 kilometres until you reach your destination.

- Take a right turn up the road, which you'll shortly leave again on the right to walk up the first old asphalted road. Just before entering Istán village, there is a signpost to the chapel of Ermita, which has a small statue of San Miguel, the patron saint of the village. Make a little detour of just a few minutes to reach the viewpoint over the lake with the information panel.

- Further on, you enter Istán at Los Altos hotel. However, if you want to finish in beauty, walk through the village towards the mirador, where you can enjoy another, but again, unique view of the lake.

- Take some well-deserved refreshment on the church-square terraces and count the number of cyclists arriving in the village!

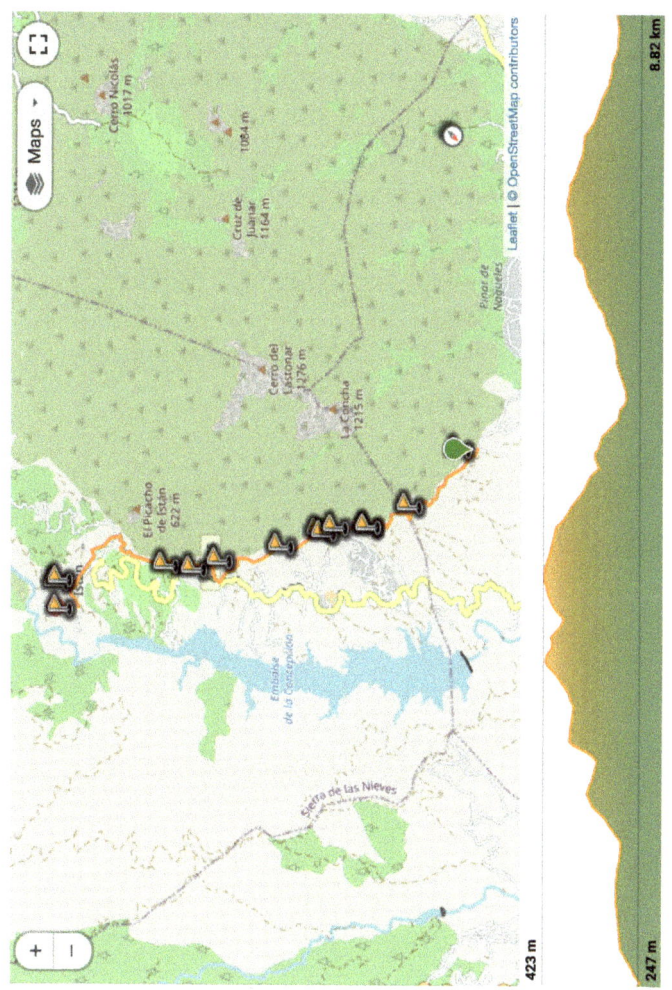

Extra walk tip: climb from Marbella promenade up to Juanar

The walk from Marbella's promenade up to Juanar is a challenging but rewarding one. This rather long linear walk is described in reverse starting from Juanar, simply because you can enjoy endless views while walking down, and without having to worry about 'how to get back down again'. Taxis are widely available and there is no need to drive up first to leave a car behind (which, of course, is a good alternative).

STARTING POINT DON MIGUEL / TRAPICHE

Driving directions to Don Miguel / Trapiche:

- On the AP-7, take exit 184 Casco antiguo/Av. Trapiche (bus station), cross the highway and drive towards the mountain until you reach the tall Hotel Don Miguel (Club Med) at the 3rd roundabout.

- **Starting Point, Xarblanca school:** Go left by the hotel (Calle Paco Padre Ostos) until the end. Turn left (Calle Doña Francisca Carrillo Doña Paquita), then first right into Avenida Florida until the end, where there is the public school and a parking. The trail starts on the road which descends at the end on the right side, next to the Mirador de Sierra Blanca urbanization.

- **Starting Point, Don Miguel**: Go right by the hotel and first left just behind it where the trail starts at the small open parking area.

WALK 6: MONKS, WATERFALLS & COASTAL VIEWS: THE 'MONJES' WALK

The facts

Type:	Circular
Length:	5.32 kilometres
Level:	Moderate
Elevation:	213 metres
Time:	2.15 hours

What to expect

Among all the beautiful mountain trails, this one may be Marbella's best kept secret at just a couple of minutes away. You'll be treated to spectacular views over Marbella's entire coastline and enjoy the small refreshing waterfalls of the Guadalpin (or Monks') river. It's a great walk to explore especially in winter and spring even after a period of heavy rain.

The trail climbs alongside the river through a pine forest until it reaches the monks' hermitage at a crest. From there it's a partly flat but mainly gentle climb along the valley with great views towards the eastern coast of Marbella. After the summit, you'll go down and enjoy far-reaching views over the west of Marbella towards Gibraltar. Then it continues through a forest and a private residential area: the Cascada de Camoján. There are some rocks along the trail and a short part where there are chains to hold on to if you want because of a steep deep slope on one side, so take a bit more care here. You also have to cross the river at several points, but all of this is fun and sounds harder than it actually is.

History, stories and more

Monks' refuge

The ruins you encounter on the hike are known as 'Los Monjes' (the Monks) hermitage and have become a reference point for walkers in the area. The Guadalpin river itself is often referred to as the Monks' river. According to legend, the Franciscan community built the hermitage in the 16th century for their prayers. The water was said to have healing powers and it is no wonder that there used to be a sacred pathway from the Incarnation church in the centre up to the hermitage. At that time, the area was still forested and the walk was not without danger given the continued presence of the Iberian wolf. However, recent clearing works suggest that the hermitage used to be a farmhouse where people actually lived, worked, and kept their livestock. Whatever future research reveals, walking your way up to the sound of tinkling waterfalls certainly boosts your well-being and relaxes the mind.

Step-by-step walking guide

- Starting point: walk left from Xarblanca School (driving directions above).

- Cross the river and turn right on the foot trail, which after a few metres continues after a big rock at the riverside in the area called Cañada de los Monjes.

- Continue along the river enjoying the waterfalls and keep following Los Monjes at the signpost.

- Cross the river and when you reach the river again, stay right.

- Cross the dried-up river.

- Continue over the rocks by the side of the rocks in river.

- Cross the dry river again.

- Cross again on your right where the trail continues.

- Cross twice more and you'll soon reach the ruins of 'Los Monjes' where other trails from Puerto Rico meet.

- The trail angles left. Keep the valley and east coast views on your left. There are some parts where you can use the chains attached to the rocks for your safety, although they aren't strictly needed.

- The trail flattens and then gently ascends to a hill opening onto the views towards the west of Marbella.

- Go down through dense pine forest again and continue until it opens up at the La Rana rest area.

- The trail ends at the residential area Cascada de Camoján, where you turn left onto the road.

- Take the first left again on Calle el Olivar until reaching a small car park with a fence and gate.

- Pass through the gate (please shut it again!) on the trail next to the deep valley, closing the loop back where you started.

WALK 7: MARBELLA'S VIEWPOINT PEAK: THE 'GITANOS' WALK

The facts

Type:	Linear
Length:	4.12 kilometres
Level:	Moderate
Elevation:	347 metres
Time:	2 hours <u>return</u>

What to expect

This is probably your closest, quickest, and steepest trail next to town. It leads to a lower peak with 360 degrees of fabulous views over the wild scenery of the Sierra Blanca mountain. However, don't let the shortness of this walk mislead you, because you gain a lot of height in no time. The summit of 'Los Gitanos' (the Gypsies) is 480 metres above sea level and its sharp peak with rocks and low vegetation guarantee excellent views. Looking inland, you can spot the cross on the mountain at Juanar (La Cruz), the Sierra Bermeja mountain towards Estepona, the Rock of Gibraltar, and the entire east/west coastline of Marbella.

At first, the walk follows a narrow pine-forest trail. Then it zigzags up the mountain with more rocks and the plants

gradually becoming shorter. In general, the walk is fairly well indicated, but some other trails cross and at these points you should pay careful attention. You can easily connect this walk with the Lighthouse trail or with the Monks' trail for a longer and more intense experience.

History, stories and more

Don Miguel hotel

This tall star-shaped building used to be the glorious Don Miguel hotel, which operated in Marbella between 1975 and 2000. It introduced the 'All-inclusive' hotel formula. Artists and hotel staff performed in an impressive theatrical setting, said to be the largest at the time in Malaga with more than 1,000 seats. At the time, this type of 'All-inclusive' tourism was in contrast to the jet-set reputation of Marbella, but the new formula was received with success. After many years of closure, the hotel is being completely restored and will give a new stimulus to this area of Marbella.

Gypsies

Los Gitanos (Gypsies/Romani) settled deeply into Spain, even though they are still mostly an isolated and not always

respected community. Their form of dance, singing, and music is said to have contributed to the famous dramatic and graceful Flamenco art form.

Step-by-step walking guide

- The route begins just behind the Hotel Don Miguel. From the roundabout in front of the complex, take the road on the right along the fence of the hotel, which is on your left. Then go left behind the hotel, where you'll find an open space to leave the car.

- Follow the dirt road that runs behind the hotel in the direction of the forest, passing the municipal water deposit on your right.

- Take the first right on the narrower trail leading into the forest and keep right on Salvador Morero until you come to the open space in the forest.

- Keep going on Salvador Morero.

- At Puerto Juan Ruiz, angle right towards S.Morero. You need to watch your feet here as the trail is a bit rocky.

- At the signpost, follow the directions to Vereda del Faro (not Pitas). There are fewer plants and views open up behind you towards Puerto Banus.

- At the next signpost, go left up to the highest Gitanos' viewpoint or right to a lower one.

Challenge Hike Tip! Combine the BUENAVISTA + MONKS' walks:

Via the GR249 route: there is a signposted trail that connects Buenavista/Nagüeles and La Rana/Nagüeles (on the Monks' walk) above the Sierra Blanca residential area. A little after the beginning of the Buenavista walk, take the direction to Ojén. On the Monks' walk, at the rest area of La Rana, do not continue on the trail straight down, but take the other trail at right-angles to it.

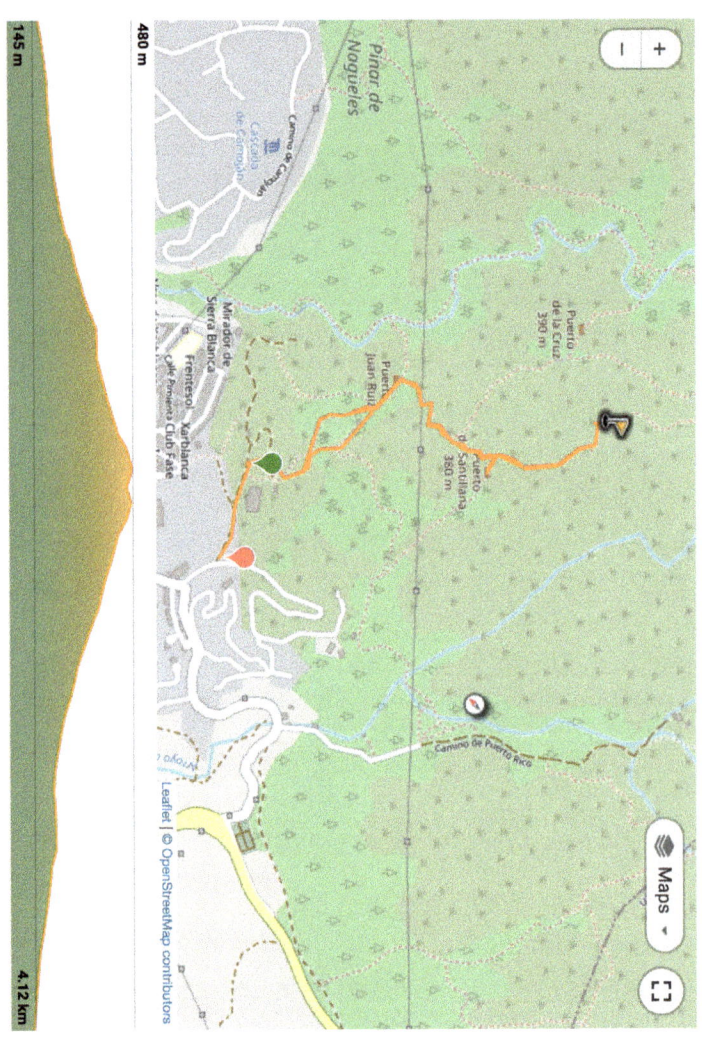

STARTING POINT PUERTO RICO / LA CAÑADA

Driving directions to Puerto Rico / La Cañada:

- On the AP-7, take the exit to Ojén behind the La Cañada shopping centre.

- Immediately turn left to the 'cementerio' (cemetery).

- Keep straight on passing the cemetery on your right and continue until you can park at a small viewpoint on your left. Start here or do the following:

- Continue opposite the viewpoint and take the old tarmac road that goes up the mountain to Puerto Rico Bajo (circa 350 meters), where there is another parking space.

- You can also reach this starting point from Don Miguel: go right by the hotel, continue on this road, which angles sharp right and reaches the small parking area at the view point.

Walk 8: Gorgeous cliffs, river and views: The Lighthouse Trail

The facts

Type:	Circular
Length:	6.78 kilometres
Level:	Moderate
Elevation:	290 metres
Time:	3 hours

What to expect

This is a lively and varied hike with rivers to cross between dense forest and climbs rewarded by stunning sea and mountain views. All of this is on the southern slope of the hilly Sierra Blanca mountain. Right from the start, you'll be wowed by the red-grey cliffs in front of you as you make your way up the Tajo Travertino plateau. Once up, the walk continues on a flatter part between scrubland and forest, and then goes up and down the valleys. There is a small more technical part where the trail is a bit rocky and runs beside a deep ravine, with superb views towards the tree-covered plateau and the Marbella coast. If you can experience this on a sunny day in spring, you can see the white blossoming almond trees like white dots on a green carpet. At the final summit, far-reaching views await you towards Puerto Banus, the Mediterranean, Gibraltar, and

Africa. This 'Vereda del Faro' (Lighthouse trail) is not widely known yet, and until it is, you can be secure in reconnecting with nature in all its tranquility.

History, stories, and more

Agriculture in the mountains

Like many other trails on the Sierra Blanca mountain, the Lighthouse trail lost its relevance for daily use and became overgrown and inaccessible. But then four entrepreneurial women and a group of volunteers came along who courageously restored and reopened the old trail. A little bit of local history was rescued by this effort because it wasn't just any trail. It used to be the most important route through the entire Puerto Rico valley, which was intensely cultivated. This explains why, in this wilderness, cultivated plants and fruit trees unexpectedly pop up. Other names that conjure up the distant past include 'Puerto de las Pitas', 'Montua', 'Puerto Rico alto', 'Los Monjes', and 'Puerto Juan Ruiz'.

Step-by-step walking guide

- Starting point: The small parking area at Puerto Rico bajo (driving directions above).
- Follow the wide pebbled trail behind the chain – you'll pass a small spring of mountain water.

- Continue straight on until the end ignoring the first right turn (you can take the next turns also). The trail gradually becomes narrower with rocks and gets a bit steeper towards the stunning reddish 'Puerto Rico' cliffs with their caves.

- Go right. This part of the trail ends at the old water pipeline and takes a 90-degree right turn.

- Zigzag your way up. A little easy mountain path will now take you up in a few minutes.

- You are now on the plateau or 'Tajo Travertino', where you'll pass the overgrown ruin of a tiny house.

- Go left in the direction of 'Puerto Rico Alto' and Juanar (right is towards Ojén).

- Only a few metres further is Puerto Rico Alto, where you go left in the direction of Puerto de las Pitas/Marbella. The trail continues through the forest, crosses a river, then climbs up on a narrower mountain trail at the edge of the valley with views towards the Tajo Travertino, which is where you came from. Once at 'Puerto del Pino', the trail goes down and then up again to the summit after crossing a river (Arroyo de las Represa).

- Follow the GR249 (red/white) trail and you'll find a signpost pointing to the fabulous viewpoint of 'Puerto de las Pitas'.

- Now make your way back down to the start at La Montua.

- Follow the same trail all the way down marked as 'La Hoya de las Golodrinas', and then 'las Papeletas'.

- At the old wooden signpost, follow the trail that turns left (do not follow the trail to Los Monjes on the right).

- Go left towards puerto Santillana and walk up (last time now!) to another summit (don't go down to Marbella).

- At the top, follow the path to La Mantua on the right, which takes you back down into the forest.
- Go across the river and straight along the wider forest trail among huge pine trees.
- Take a 90-degree right turn onto a smaller track, which almost immediately connects you to the upper car park with the chain.

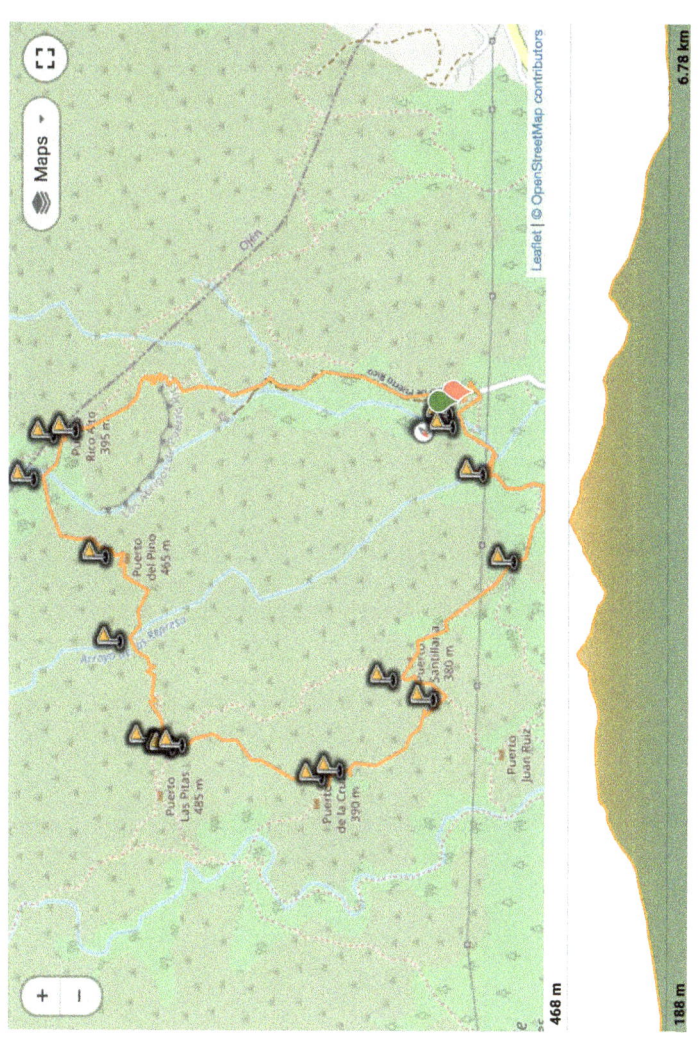

Walk 9: Children's Mountain Circuit up Tajo Travertino

The facts

Type:	Circular
Length:	3.65 kilometres
Level:	Easy
Elevation:	213 metres
Time:	1.5 hours

What to expect

This short circular walk is a good introduction to hiking in the Sierra Blanca for children. The elevation gain is gradual, you get in touch with nature, and enjoy views over Marbella's coast.

Children can have a good time especially in the winter months. For example, at the start they can see the impressive gap in the rock, and further on, splash in the trails wetted by a gentle mountain river. In spring, the plateau is of extraordinary beauty, with the white blossoms of the almond trees colouring the mountain. Summers are hot, so, as with all hikes, an early rise, abundant water, and sun protection are a must.

History, stories and more

Marble

The rocks are formed of travertine, which is a beautiful beige natural stone that has been intensively exploited for building, including flooring, bathrooms, fireplaces, and decorative purposes. This cool marble-like stone has long been a welcome feature in houses during the warm summer months.

Step-by-step walking guide

- Starting point: The small parking area at Puerto Rico bajo (driving directions above).

- Follow the wider pebbled trail behind the chain – you'll pass a small spring of mountain water.

- Continue straight on to the end ignoring the right turn to Ojén. The trail gradually becomes narrower with rocks and a bit steeper towards the stunning reddish 'Puerto Rico' cliffs with their caves.

- Go right. This part of the trail ends at the old water pipeline and takes a 90-degree right turn.

- Zigzag your way up. A little easy mountain path will now take you up in a few minutes.

- You are now on the plateau or 'Tajo Travertino', where you'll pass the overgrown ruin of a tiny house.

- Take a right turn, following the signpost to Ojén. You'll walk between tall plants on a flat sandy trail over the plateau, then gradually go down again into the pine forest on a rockier trail.

- Go right at the next turn – signposted 'Marbella'– and make your way down.

- Go left at the end. The trail ends at the wide pebbled trail where your walk started.

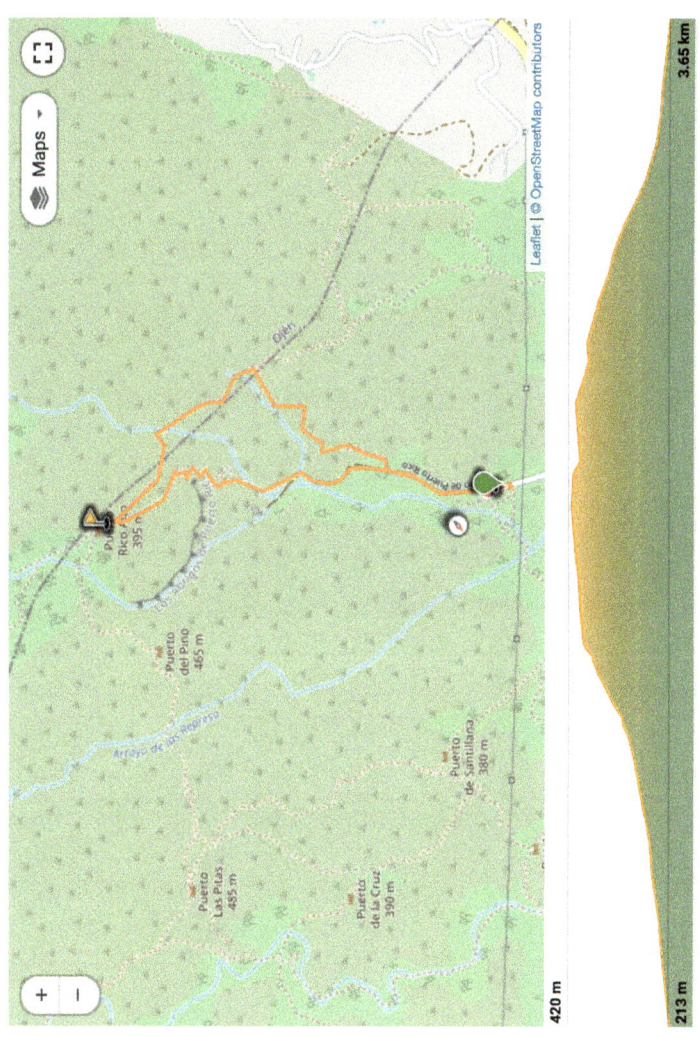

WALK 10: MARBELLA TO THE WHITE VILLAGE OF OJÉN

The facts

Type:	Linear (leave a car at Ojén for your return!)
Length:	9.30 kilometres
Level:	Moderate
Elevation:	503 metres
Time:	3 hours one-way

What to expect

This is a scenic mountain walk from Marbella that gently climbs on the south and east side of the mountain towards its rewarding destination, the picturesque white village of Ojén. After a short dip into the forest, views open up towards the east coast of Marbella and then over the valleys towards Ojén. The hike is pretty straightforward, with (normally) no surprises, and follows a generally well-indicated trail. Only a very small part of the trail is narrow at the side of a steep valley slope.

Once you approach Ojén, you'll soon realize this isn't a quiet sleepy village, but a rather busy even noisy place where every little townhouse seems to be undergoing refurbishment or getting a new coat of paint. If you would like to complete this wonderful walking experience in a serene atmosphere, have a little peep into the church on the main square with its lovely flowers, fountain, and inviting terraces.

History, stories and more

Fit fishermen

Not so long ago, local fishermen (without hiking shoes and gear) would walk up the mountain from Marbella to Ojén in the very early morning hours to deliver the freshly caught fish of the day.

Mining railway

When mining was big in the 19th century, the dirt road at the beginning of this walk used to be a mining railway from Ojén to Marbella. It was built by the English 'Marbella Iron Ore Company', which reopened the previously successful 'Mina del Peñoncillo' (Peñoncillo mine). Iron-ore was so abundant in the mountain that at one time production represented almost 70% of the national iron output. Later, in 1957, a monocable was installed to transport the mineral directly to the cargo ships moored offshore at Torre del Cable, just behind the current industrial park of Marbella.

Step-by-step walking guide

- Starting point: The small parking area on the road to Puerto Rico bajo (driving directions above).

- Go right uphill on the gravel road behind the chain.
- At the first turn close by, take the first right into a narrower forest trail, following the signpost to Hoya de los Cabañiles. The trail zigzags up the mountain slope among pine trees, a variety of short plants, and beautiful blooming flowers. It runs parallel to a river.
- At the next signpost (Number 46), you take a right turn towards Ojén. The climb continues, where you are treated to magnificent panoramic views of Marbella towards Puerto Banus.
- At the next signpost (Number 47), you take a left turn, where you can view eastern Marbella and, further on the trail, the port close to the town centre. Go up and down a little, and walk towards an open green valley with some beehives in the distance and, once again, open views to the east and the entire coast.
- Once you reach the valley, go left and walk along it with sea views on your right. The walk is now pretty flat and easy until it gradually climbs again and enters the forest by the fence of an older luxurious residential area (which, surprisingly, includes a private bull ring). It gradually goes down on a mountain path where you'll have your first views of Ojén. You'll be treated to these view many a time, but there are still some valleys to walk through before reaching the village.
- You'll cross a charming stream and further up you'll find a rectangular water basin, where you go left. IMPORTANT! Don't go right, even though this way also goes to Ojén. It is extremely dangerous, because you have to cross a stream with a ravine. The correct trail now goes on a narrow mountain path next to a deep valley slope to your right.
- Continue towards the mobile-telephone masts, where the trail changes into a wider dirt road that is accessible to cars. Continue straight down the hill until you reach

the road. Keeping to the left, enter the tunnel under the road and go down to the village. Astonishingly, this village includes a large number of sports facilities that many villages can only dream of. Walk further down by the side of these facilities. Take a break and, once again, enjoy the different viewpoints, where you have a better view of the red-grey caves and cliffs on which Ojén is built. You now reach the upper part of the town close to the petrol station. Visit the cave and the breath-taking viewpoint over the village before meandering into the steep narrow village streets towards the big car park at the bottom.

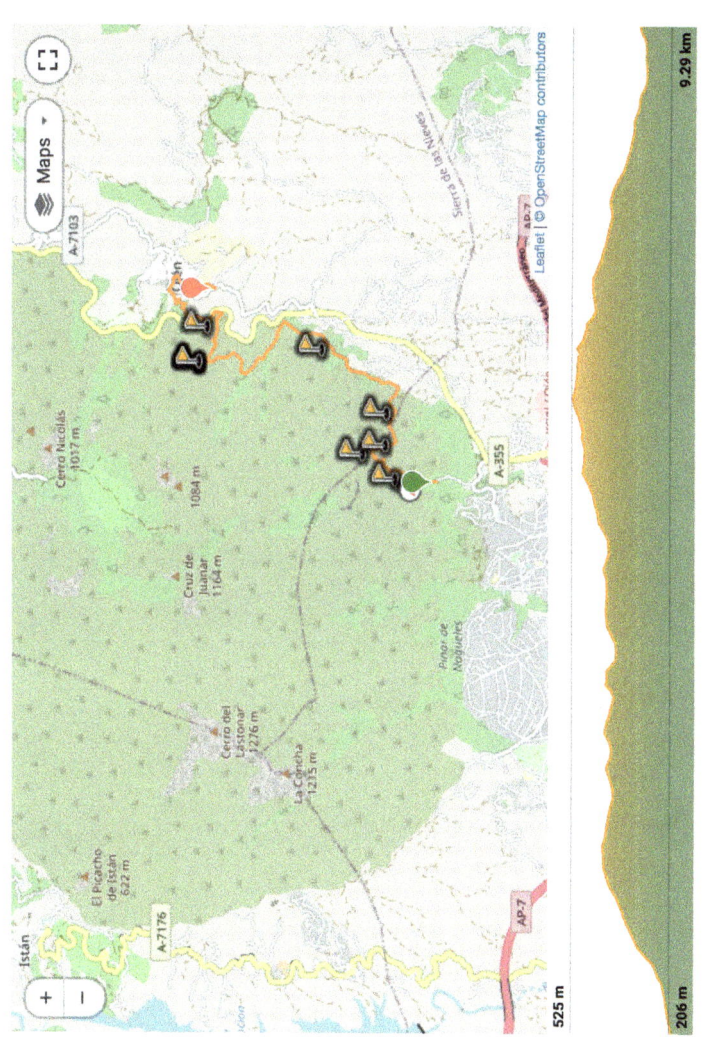

WALK 11: STRAIGHT UP TO THE VIEWPOINT TERRACE MONTÉS OF JUANAR

The facts

Type:	Linear
Length:	11.26 kilometres
Level:	Moderate
Elevation:	714 metres
Time:	4 hours return

What to expect

Boost your cardio level with this hike, which runs in an almost straight line up the southern slope of the Sierra Blanca. Fortunately, you won't have to search for the way too much, because this trail is well indicated, easily accessible, and flattens out on some stretches. You'll be treated to a variety of sensations; the feeling of the dense forest and the sound of the river flowing, views of the red-grey cone-shaped rocks rising above the green slopes in the distance, and panoramas of the peak of La Cruz and the coast of central Marbella. The first, and steepest, part goes towards the plateau with the red-grey rocks. The path gets easier as it runs through the forest and then views open up as you climb. Apart from the climb itself from 212 metres to 913 metres, your only challenge is your level of

cardio-fitness as this walk has no technical aspects or 'scary parts with ravines'. As ever, your effort will be rewarded when you reach the fabulous paved terrace viewpoint of Juanar.

History, stories and more

Viewpoint towards Marbella

You'll walk from Marbella into the municipality of Ojén where the lodge and entrance to Juanar natural park is located. After walking in complete wilderness, surprisingly, a very well-maintained paved viewpoint awaits you at 900 metres. This is a rustic balcony with spectacular views overlooking the Mediterranean, from which you can enjoy the colourful play of the green mountains, the white Marbella town, and the blue sea. Beautiful and much-loved Iberian mountain goats, or ibex, can very often be spotted here. The mountain is their natural habitat, as the name of the viewpoint evokes: 'Mirador del Macho Montés' (the viewpoint of the male wild mountain goat). A statue of this beautiful male ibex proudly stands on the rocks above the terrace and it is truly magical to see it surrounded by real goats. Keep your camera ready!

Step-by-step walking guide

- Starting point: at the small parking area at Puerto Rico bajo (driving directions above).

- Follow the wide pebbled trail behind the chain – you'll pass a small spring of mountain water on the right.

- Continue straight on until the end ignoring the right turn to Ojén. The trail gradually becomes narrower with rocks and gets a bit steeper towards the stunning reddish 'Puerto Rico' cliffs with their caves.

- Turn right in front of the tiny construction This part of the trail ends at the old waterpipe and takes a 90-degree right turn onto a mountain trail.

- Zigzag your way up. A little easy mountain path will now take you up in a few minutes.

- The trail gets flatter and continues onto the plateau or 'Tajo Travertino', where you'll pass the overgrown ruin of a tiny house.

- Go left in the direction of 'Puerto Rico Alto' and Juanar (right is towards Ojén). The trail now runs through pine forest.

- At 'Puerto Rico Alto' continue straight up towards Juanar. At the next turn just keep going towards Juanar until you reach the summit with the 'Mirador del Macho Montés' viewpoint. This walk is linear, so just walk back the way you came.

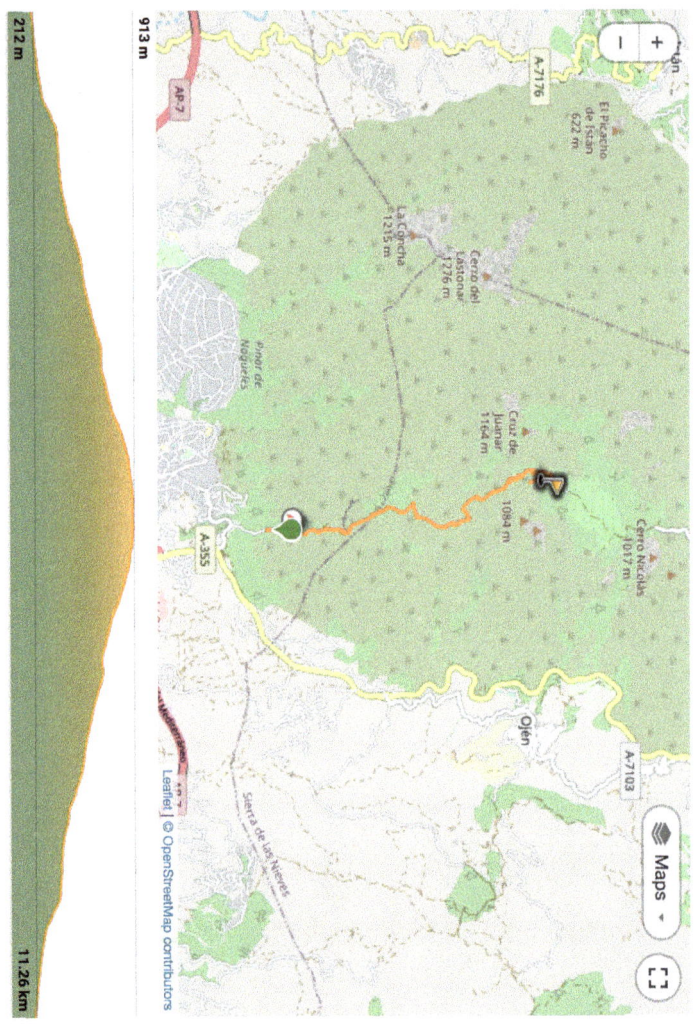

Longer hike tip:

1) By connecting up with walk Number 9, as described previously, you could climb up to the peak of La Cruz de Juanar. This option would add another 1.5 to 2 hours to the walk.

2) Instead of taking the same way back, you can follow the trail to Juan Benitéz, as indicated on the first signpost, and then go towards Puerto Rico alto.

STARTING POINT: UP ON THE MOUNTAIN AT JUANAR

Driving directions

- It's around a 20-minute drive from Marbella to Juanar.

- On the AP-7, take the Ojén exit (A-355) behind the La Cañada shopping centre. Stay on this scenic road and pass Ojén.

- After Ojén, the road gets flatter where the first left turn goes to 'Refugio Juanar'. Follow this until the end (around 10 minutes), where you arrive at the car park (and the lodge on the street on the right).

- Walk up to the entrance gates to the park. There is also some limited parking space in front of the gates.

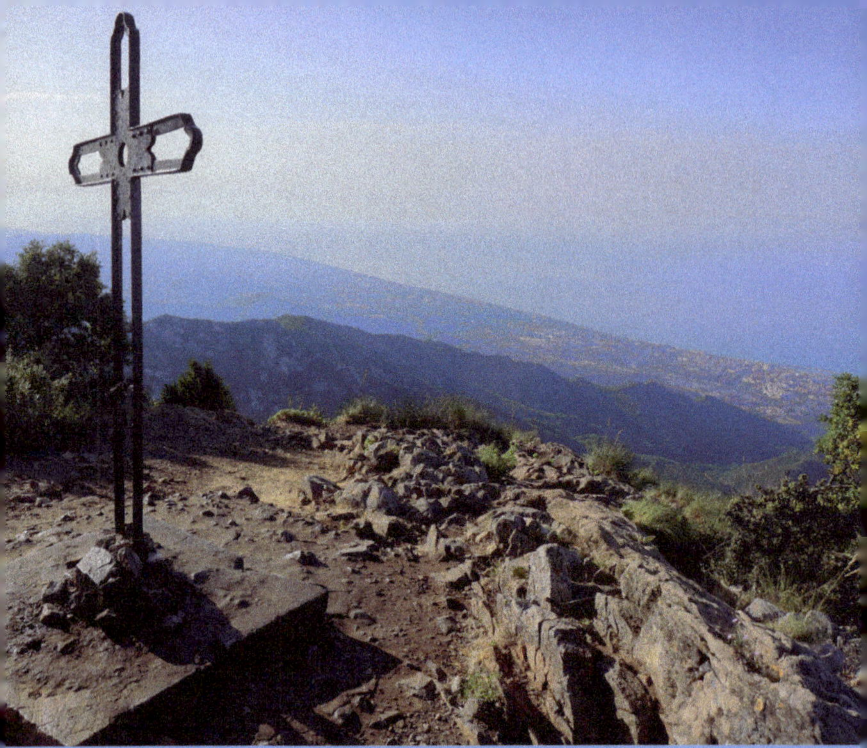

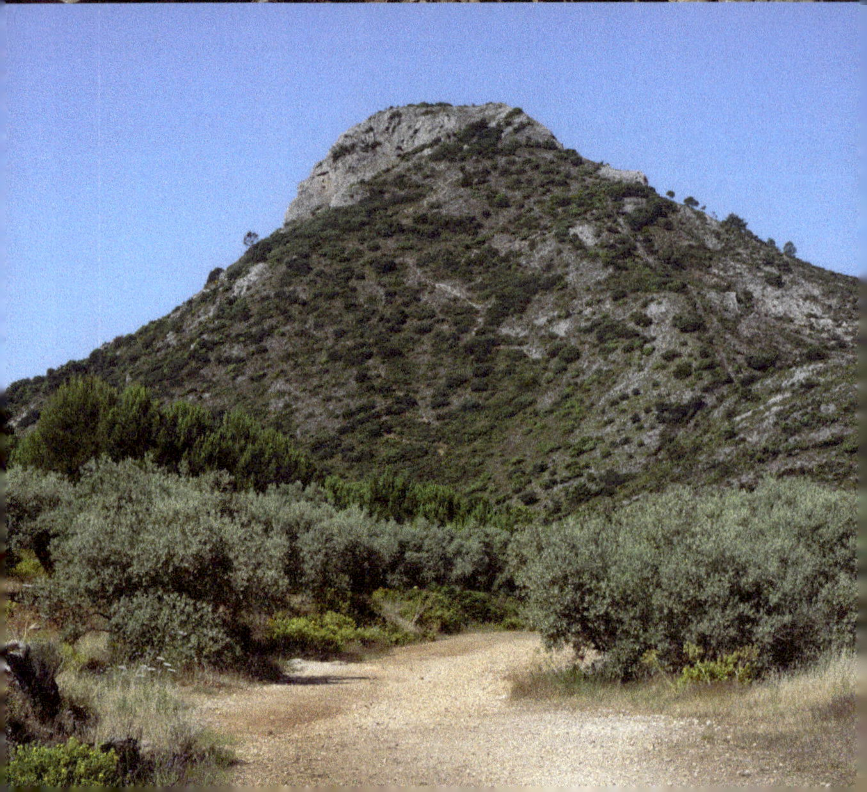

WALK 12: OLIVE TREES, PINE FOREST AND CLIMB TO THE PEAK OF LA CRUZ

The facts

Type:	Circular
Length:	6.15 kilometres
Level:	Moderate
Elevation:	349 metres
Time:	2-2.5 hours

What to expect

This walk is an ideal first choice to explore the Sierra Blanca mountain scenery from Juanar. After a gradual climb on a wide forest trail between enormous pine and chestnut trees, the trail levels out at a plateau covered with olive trees: the 'Olivar de Juanar'. This part is very easy and popular with families over the weekend. The next part is on a gradually ascending forestry trail which reaches a plateau ('Las Allanás'), where the final part to La Cruz begins with a steeper climb until you reach the peak at 1,184 metres. At the metal cross on the summit, there's enough space to take a break and to soak up the breathtaking 360-degree view. The trail goes down the other side on a zigzagging trail with lots of rocks and short plants, providing views towards the olive-tree plateau where you came from. This hike is very scenic and full of variety. You could take on a

two-summit hike by doing this walk in reverse and continuing to the further and challenging peak of La Concha (another 3 hours!).

History, stories and more

Saved by the Virgin

According to legend, the metal cross, which was originally made of wood, was raised there by some fishermen in gratitude to la Virgen del Carmen (the Virgin Carmen), who answered their desperate prayers while sailing a stormy sea fearing for their lives. Suddenly, after praying, the sea calmed down and they could see the peak of the mountain, helping them to sail back home. The current iron cross, which you can see from far away, has become a landmark of the mountain. There's also a tiny shrine with the Virgin and Child placed next to it. This miracle is celebrated every year in May on the traditional Día de la Cruz (Day of the Cross), when people, including some elderly ones, walk their way up to make a wish and attend mass.

Step-by-step walking guide

- From the entrance of Juanar, follow the wide forest trail behind the gates. This takes you up to the plateau of olive trees (Olivar de Juanar).

- Viewpoint: at the start of the plateau, there is a small trail that goes left to the Corzo viewpoint (if you want to do this part, add an extra 40 minutes there and back again).

- At the end of the plateau, the trail goes left at the turn. Instead, take a right turn here and go between the olive trees. The trail narrows a little at this part.

- At the next turn, keep left following signpost 'La Concha'.

- A few minutes on, angle left and continue towards 'La Concha'. The trail is still wide and gradually starts going up between big pine trees and ferns.

- After an open space, the walk becomes steeper on a narrow trail until you reach the first summit at Puerto de las Allanás.

- Go left here to zigzag up above the forest. Here and

there you have to take big steps on the stones, but you soon reach the summit with the viewpoint and cross.

- La Cruz (The Cross) viewpoint is on your right – enjoy splendid views!

- Go down the trail on the other side of the summit, where you have to be a bit careful because of the rocks and stones. Red arrows have been painted on the rocks to help you find the path. In the distance, you can see the olive grove and forest you are heading to.

- Once down at the forest, a left turn reconnects you with the olive-tree plateau. Make your way back down, but before returning, take a break at the viewpoint 'Mirador Macho Montés' on your right.

Long Hike Tip:

1) Start at Ojén village, hike up to Juanar, and connect with the La Cruz walk.

2) Start at Puerto Rico, walk up to the Macho Montés viewpoint, and continue to La Cruz.

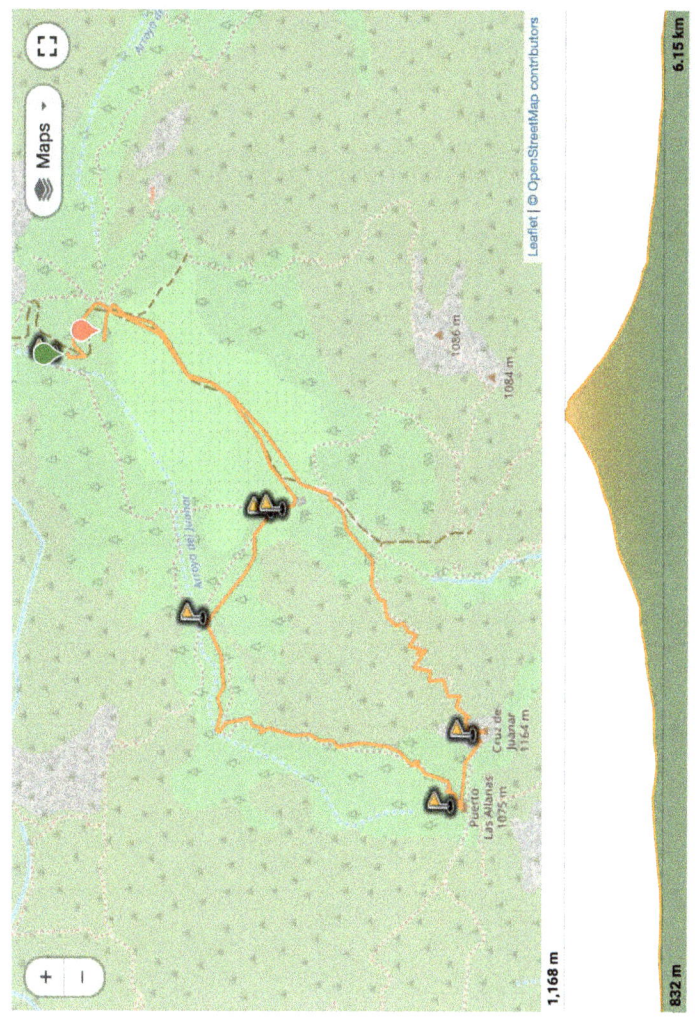

WALK 13: FOR HIKING EXPERTS: A NOT-TO-BE-MISSED HIKE UP TO THE PEAK OF LA CONCHA

The facts

Type:	Linear
Length:	13.69 kilometres
Level:	Hard
Elevation:	743 metres
Time:	6 hours return

What to expect

'You haven't walked the Sierra Blanca, if you haven't reached La Concha'. The walk up to the peak of La Concha at 1,215 meters is a must for every passionate hiker. The summit has 360-degree views as far as the eyes can see: the African coast and mainland, the Istán lake, and the other challenging summit of Torrecilla. The trail is well indicated towards the first summit plateau of Las Allanás, but once you pass this part, you must pay careful attention. The walk is rated hard because it is quite tricky, with narrow stony trails and deep dangerous ravines. At a specific point, you have to use a chain attached to the cliff. However, despite these risky sections, the trail is not

only popular with experienced hikers, but also with teenagers and families with children. IMPORTANT! This walk is not recommended if you have a fear of heights or are unfit.

History, stories and more

Let it snow...

Although rare, it can snow in Marbella. When it does, the emblematic peak of La Concha can stay white for up to a couple of days, providing unique shots for photographers. Stick to photography on these days and don´t walk up to the summit.

...but not burn

Forest fires in Spain are common, although most are small and controllable. However, in 2012, an unprecedented shock went through the entire coast when strong winds made a wildfire rage out of control. Thousands of hectares of land were burned and forced the evacuation of 4,000 people, including some from residential areas in Marbella as well as the entire village of Ojén. For days, more than 400 fire fighters and members of the armed forces helped to tame the flames. Even the residents of less-threatened areas at the foot of the mountains, including the Sierra Blanca, will never forget the smell of burning and the rain of ashes covering their houses, gardens, pools, and terrace furniture.

Important information

This challenging walk has been described elsewhere, signposted, and mapped with all the best of intentions. However, what has not been sufficiently emphasized is that this walk is not without risk. The mountain can be treacherous and the climate even more so. Unfortunately, every year, firefighters have to rescue people who have got lost, been (seriously) injured, suffered heatstroke, or have even burned down a part of the precious forest by starting a fire. Make sure you are fully equipped, fit enough for the hike, and leave on time. Providing you fulfil these essentials, without any doubt whatsoever, this walk will amaze you!

Step-by-step walking guide

- It is advisable to download the map of the area and use a mobile app to follow the trail.
- From the entrance of Juanar, follow the wide forest trail which takes you up to the plateau of olive trees.
- At the end of the plateau, the trail goes left at the turn. Instead, take a right turn into the olive trees. The trail

narrows and starts going up in the pine forest.

- Keep left at the next turn, where the trail gradually climbs and gets steeper towards the first summit (Puerto de las Allanás).

- At this summit you have your first views of the sea. Turn right (left is towards La Cruz) and follow the trail through oak trees. It soon angles right. You have to watch your steps here because of the rocks and the narrow stretch next to a deep ravine.

- After a stretch of flat land, the climb begins and you can spot the highest peak of Lastonar. Keep a close eye out for the piled-up stones. There's a risky bit where you need to take a very big step (use your hands if it feels safer). The locals call this 'El salto del lobo' (The wolves' jump).

- The trail now gets very narrow with an almost vertical wall on one side making a fall very dangerous. Even so, you can pass this easily providing you take care.

- The climb continues until a small open area where you can rest before passing through another tricky area. Fortunately, there are chains to help you pass, which makes it fairly safe. However, it is definitely not recommended if you have vertigo.

- Follow the ridge as the trail is now not clear, but footprints can help. Continue until the signpost to Istán. You can see the shell-shaped peak from here. Keep following the ridge towards the peak. The way is indicated with red and blue markings until you are almost there.

- There is a bench at the peak to sit, relax, and have a snack before retracing your steps.

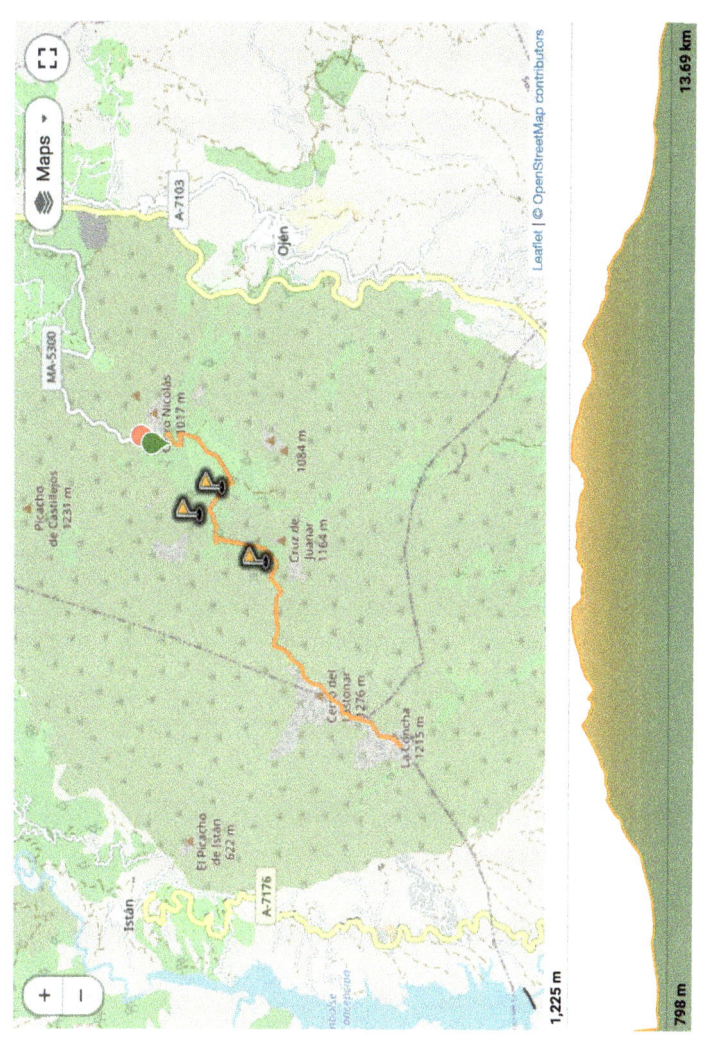

Walk 14: From high up in Juanar down to Marbella promenade: valleys & views

The facts

Type:	Linear
Length:	12 kilometres
Level:	Hard
Elevation:	1000 metres
Time:	5 hours one-way

What to expect

The starting and finishing points of this walk couldn't be more different. From the solitude of the mountain to the busy coastal town, you'll feel a little out of place in your hiking gear once in central Marbella!

The walk is rated physically hard due to its length, but not for its difficulty because it runs along quite easy accessible mountain trails that go up and down three valleys. But just for a change, it starts at the top.

Over the complete walk, you'll be treated to spectacular views over the coastline in its entirety. Nevertheless, more views means more sun exposure, so please be prepared.

This is a linear walk that is ideal for those looking for a more

intense challenge. It is also an example of how you can connect the different trails and crossing points on the mountain.

History, stories and more

Ruin of the Casa de la Guarda & Refugio

This ruin was one of three houses in the Sierra Blanca that belonged to José Aurelio de Larios, the 3rd Marquess of Larios, who used them to house his security staff and their families.

The houses were close to his 'Refugio' (hunting lodge), which he built in 1906 in the middle of the mountain at 780 metres. Alfonso XIII visited the lodge as one of his guests, thus making its opening official. The lodge was later abandoned, but in 1965 the Larios family generously donated it along with the entire Sierra Blanca mountain to the state. It then was included in the list of national paradors, which are a type of luxury hotel located in converted historic buildings. It became emblematic for its outstanding peaceful and isolated natural location, and was frequented by famous figures such as Charles de Gaulle. Since then, the hotel has just about managed to stay open.

Step-by-step walking guide

- Don't forget, this walk is linear. Leave a car at the end of the walk in Nagüeles (Marbella) at the entrance of the Cascada de Camoján residential area or at the Palacio de Congresos in Marbella if you want to walk down all the way (this option is 30-minutes longer than the walk described above).

- Start at Juanar. Walk through the park's entrance gate just above the hunting lodge. The first 15 minutes will lead you through a pine and chestnut tree forest.

- The trail then opens up onto a sun-exposed plateau covered with olive trees: the 'Olivar de Juanar'. After around 200 metres, almost at the end of this flat area, there is a signpost pointing towards the forest trails on the right leading to La Cruz, La Concha, and Istán. Instead, continue left towards the viewpoint or 'Mirador Macho Montés'.

- Just before the viewpoint, turn immediately right at the signpost indicating the way to Marbella. But before going that way, enjoy the panoramic terrace, where you are already treated to the first views of Marbella. Now you have an idea of how the descent will be.

- The trail now goes down the southern slope of the mountain. Gradually zigzagging, continue and ignore the first signpost to Juan Benitez. At the next signpost indicating 'Casa del Guarda', take a right turn and follow this. You will cross a river. The trail now goes up again to the ruin of la Guarda then it flattens.

- At the next signpost, follow the direction to the Calaña valley, descending on the left and ascending on the next valley where you walk straight at the Puerto de la Adelfilla.

- The trail continues on the left towards Marbella. At the next two signposts, keep following the trail in the direction of Marbella. At the following signpost, cross the river and you'll come to the ruin of the 'Ermita las Monjes'.

- Continue straight on Nagueles. There is a steeper part on the slope where you need to take a bit more care, but there are chains to help you, although they are not strictly needed. The trail gradually goes up to the next lower summit leading to the final stretch of the walk all the way down into Marbella. On the way down, you re-enter a pine forest, where you keep left at an open area. (A right turn here would take you behind a residential area towards Nagüeles Park).

- The narrow trail on the left goes down through the forest until it ends on the asphalted road at the top of the Cascada de Camoján residential area.

- Here take a right turn, pass the reservoir, and make your way down staying on the same road until you reach your car at the entrance of this residential area. Alternatively, walk all the way straight down to the centre of the town at the Piruli (Copper Tower) or Palacio de Congreso (another 3 kilometres).

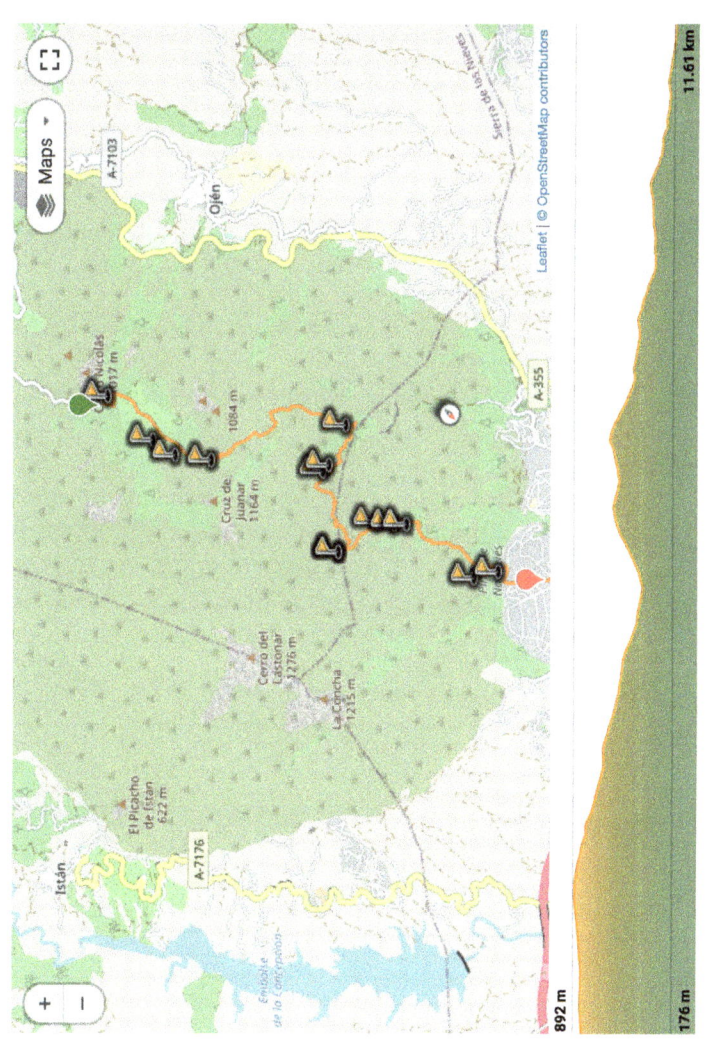

Part 2: White mountain villages close to Marbella: Ojén, Monda, Istán and Benahavis

Only a stone's throw away from Marbella there's a very different world to explore. In less than 20-minutes' drive inland, the densely-built coast gradually transforms into a colourful play of rocks, mountains, and rivers. In this almost unspoilt natural setting lie the tiny white-washed picturesque 'pueblos' or villages of Ojén, Monda, Istán, and Benahavis. Their proximity to the coast has given them a rather special character. On the one hand, Spanish local village life seems untouched, with old people chatting on benches and loud mopeds and small old cars chasing through narrow steep streets. On the other hand, foreigners have built houses and flats in and around these villages over the years and with them came more restaurants, tapas bars, and tourist lodgings in the area. But luckily the village feel, look, and life remain mostly intact. Their closeness to Marbella has also kept them relevant, connected, and very attractive for tourism. Work and top-notch facilities in Marbella are within reach, which in turn stimulates rural living and economies. These small bustling villages are doing well in contrast to many inland Spanish pueblos that have become depopulated.

Sierra de las Nieves National Park

Monda, Istán, and Ojén really have the best of two worlds. They are located in the foothills of the Sierra Blanca mountain. They also belong to a group of nine white villages that are geographically set in the Sierra de las Nieves. The very diverse ecological system, fauna, and flora in this national park have received protection as a UNESCO biosphere reserve. It's a natural paradise of topographic contrasts including gorges, peaks, cliffs, and a complex labyrinth of hidden caves.

The symbols of the region are the mountain goat and the unique 'pinsapo'. This tree is the oldest type of Mediterranean fir and the most widespread in the Sierra de las Nieves, Sierra

Bermeja, and Sierra Grazalema. The Sierra de las Nieves also hosts an impressive variety of 1,500 different types of plants and trees including many oaks, pines, and chestnuts. The area is of great interest for bird fans, as there are about 120 species of birds. Among these are the impressive day and night raptors, which can be easily spotted on a walk. Typical vegetation on the mountain slopes are shrubs and buckthorn bushes.

Apart from Istán, Ojén, and Monda, the other villages in the Sierra de las Nieves are Alozaina, Casarabonela, El Burgo, Guaro, Tolox, and Yunquera. So, there's a profusion of places for exploring and hiking, not to mention tasting the delicious local dishes! All these villages are connected by a route that can be walked in a few days, but this is beyond the scope of this book.

The highest peak in this mostly limestone mountainous region is the pale-grey Torrecilla at 1,919 metres, and the walk to the summit should definitely be on the list of any advanced hiker who visits this beautiful region. The drive to the start is a little longer than others: we describe the walk in the next section. It can be done in every season and it is not rare for the higher parts to be covered in snow during colder winter months. Don't be misled by a sunny winter day on the coast, because the temperature can drop massively up on the mountain despite its proximity to the sea resort of Marbella.

Finally, it's a National Park

Until recently, the Sierra de las Nieves was a natural park, but has just been recognized as a national park, which is a big step up. This makes it the third national park in Andalucía, along with Doñana and the Sierra Nevada. The new status should increase tourism in the area and contribute to its economic development by bringing in new jobs and businesses. It could even mean that people could work and live again in the more isolated villages that are becoming depopulated.

It will stand out as a national park because of its fir forest, which forms 65% of all firs nationwide. Other attractions include peridotite, which is a dense igneous rock and one of the rarest in the earth's crust. And of course, there's always the marvellous diversity of habitats and fauna. For example, it's the only place in Europe where you can find the 'meloncillo' or Egyptian mongoose.

Hamlet-like villages

When the Catholic Kings took over Marbella and the surrounding region in 1485, they gave the existing community of Moors or Hispano-Muslims three options: They could stay and convert to Christianity, leave Marbella to live inland, or return to North Africa. The Hispanic-Muslims who renounced their religion were called the 'Moriscos' (or New Christians) and the ones who kept it were the 'Mudéjars'. However, the Moriscos continued to maintain their traditions over time. The restrictions on them became more severe, even unbearable, leading to the Revolt of the Moriscos in 1568 during the reign of Philip II. After this, their properties were confiscated and the villages were repopulated by bringing in Christians from different parts of Spain. It all ended when King Philip III gave the harsh order to expel them from Spain in 1613.

2.1. Ojén today: 'the' place to live

Just behind the busy shopping mall of La Cañada in Marbella, you can find the road that leads to Ojén at just under 10 kilometres away. Leaving the buzz of the coast behind, you'll suddenly find yourself cutting through serene green mountain hills. After some sharp bends, the white houses of Ojén appear in the distance, tumbling up the tranquil mountain slope like a white blanket. The village is situated between the Sierra Blanca and Sierra Alpujata and nestles at around 200 metres by the Almadán stream above the Rio Real valley. Juanar is the entry point for many walks on the Sierra Blanca mountain and is located in the municipality of Ojén. Ojén is also the first and closest entry point from the coast into the magnificent Sierra de las Nieves national park. In addition, Ojén's proximity to the sea ensures a mild climate which is unlike that of most other mountain villages. In a world threatened by climate change and pollution, this perfect mix of ingredients has caught the attention of project developers who saw the potential to attract overseas buyers. The village remained unspoilt for a long time, but is now undergoing considerable changes with new residential high-end construction on the hills. Of course, this combination of attractive features had to be discovered one day, particularly because other residential areas within the Marbella municipality are much further away from its shops, facilities, and beaches. Ojén is now becoming absorbed into Marbella's fame and lifestyle. In fact, in 2015, Ojén was rated as one of the 50 best places to live worldwide according to a survey conducted by the widely read British newspaper 'The Times'. At the drop of a hat, Ojén found itself among prestigious cities such as Rome and Paris. As a result, Ojén will be receiving economic and socio-demographic aid and the current population of about 3800 residents is predicted to grow exponentially in the coming years. Only the future will tell.

Cultural heritage

If you wander around the steep winding streets, you'll encounter some charming historical features like the main

square's rectangular fountain in which water has been flowing since 1905. But the small church, Nuestra Señora de la Encarnación, takes the centre stage. It was built in 1505, incorporating an ancient mosque despite the initial promise by the Christians to respect the Moorish people. The minaret is still preserved and used as a bell tower.

In the lower part of the village, close to the big parking area, you can find a small renovated Oil Mill dating from 1800. Now a museum, it contains some original machinery and shows how oil used to be extracted from olives. There's also a Wine Museum in an old liquor distillery providing evidence of the area's quite prosperous past as a wine-making region up to the 19th century.

WALK 15: OJÉN VILLAGE TO THE EL CORZO VIEWPOINT

The Facts

Type:	Linear, partly circular
Length:	11.23 kilometres
Level:	Moderate
Elevation gain:	605 metres
Time:	4 hours

What to expect

After warming up your muscles by walking up the steep village streets (the Ojén locals must be fit!), you enter the protected wild world of the Sierra Blanca mountain. This side of the mountain is less visited and on a weekday you might be entirely on your own. The path initially runs through a dense pine and oak forest and then opens up with views to the rugged mountain. It's quite a steep climb until it ends at the plateau of Juanar. Many walks go through this part, so you may come across more people. The walk then continues at Juanar until you reach El Corzo, a great viewpoint where you can see Ojén in the distance.

History, stories and more

Caves

After the walk, take time to truly discover Ojén. There are many lovely spots to visit, including its caves. In 2005, the Cueva de las Campanas (Cave of the Bells) and the Cueva de las Columnas (Cave of the Pillars) were restored and opened to the public. You can find them in the upper part of the village and can be accessed from Calle Carretera. They are examples of the many caves in the region that are said to have been used as shelters by people and their livestock. The caves in the lower part of the village have been cleverly promoted by the town hall for concerts and events, which are growing in popularity. Higher up, the Cave of the Pillars provides a breathtaking viewpoint down towards Ojén and the sea. So, it's definitely worthwhile taking the steep stairs up to this terrace.

El Corzo

The paved El Corzo terrace offers amazing views of Ojén's location in the mountains and of the Mijas and Fuengirola coastline. You can also see the peak of La Cruz from this viewpoint. Below the terrace, look for the curious statue of a roe deer between the plants. This statue is a homage to this rare autochthonous mountain species. Its numbers have dropped in recent years, so it won't be easy to spot a real one.

Driving directions

On the AP-7, take the exit onto the A355 in the direction of Ojén. Then turn off towards Ojén and follow this road all the

way down, taking a right at the roundabout, until you reach the village car park.

Step-by-step walking guide

- Leave the large car park and make your way up the village by the Ayuntamiento (Townhall), which is clearly visible from the car park.

- Turn left at the church, which has ivy with lovely yellow flowers.

- Behind the fountain, with the church at your back, continue on the left until you reach the main road (Calle Carretera). This is the location of the caves and viewpoint.

- Keep going left towards the Repsol petrol station. Just before the station, leave the road on the opposite side to go up a short steep walkway leading to a mountain path with signposts to Istán and Monda. The hike now continues on the narrow stony forest path that turns into a wider old tarmac road. Keep walking along until the road meets another one.

- Angle left on the rocky path through the forest. In a few minutes you'll reach a tunnel under the road. The tunnel is completely dark, but don't worry because you can see the end just 20 metres ahead.

- The forest path up takes you to a gate with a door. This path is used by locals to reach the Ermita (hermitage). Walk through it to enter the nature reserve. The path is now easy to follow and continues up in the middle of a forest of mainly pine trees.

- When you reach a turn, angle left. Bit by bit, you'll catch glimpses of the stunning mountain ridges that await you. The hike ends at the Juanar plateau of olive trees. The way to the mountain hotel is on your right (15 minutes away).

- However, just before the way to the mountain hotel, go left on a narrow path and walk towards the nearby and utterly beautiful Mirador Corzo viewpoint. Have a well-deserved rest here and enjoy 360 degrees of stunning views to la Cruz, Ojén itself, and the coast in the distance.

- Walk back to where you came from, until you reach the turn. To avoid going all the way back on the same path, we go left here to take a different path back. Further down, you'll have to pass through a tunnel again, but it's a smaller one with more light, which opens up into Ojén's botanical gardens. On the right is the way out. Go through the gates, then head left or right again back into the village, and go down through the zigzagging streets to the start of the hike.

Tip

Walk 10 from Marbella to Ojén can be done in reverse starting from the village.

- Juanar connection. As this walk goes to Juanar, you can easily connect it up with all the paths that start or finish there (see previous chapter). If you go for this option, you can easily add hours of walking by hiking up to the peak of La Cruz or visit the Montés viewpoint. You could also walk back to Marbella or, for experts, hike the peak of La Concha.

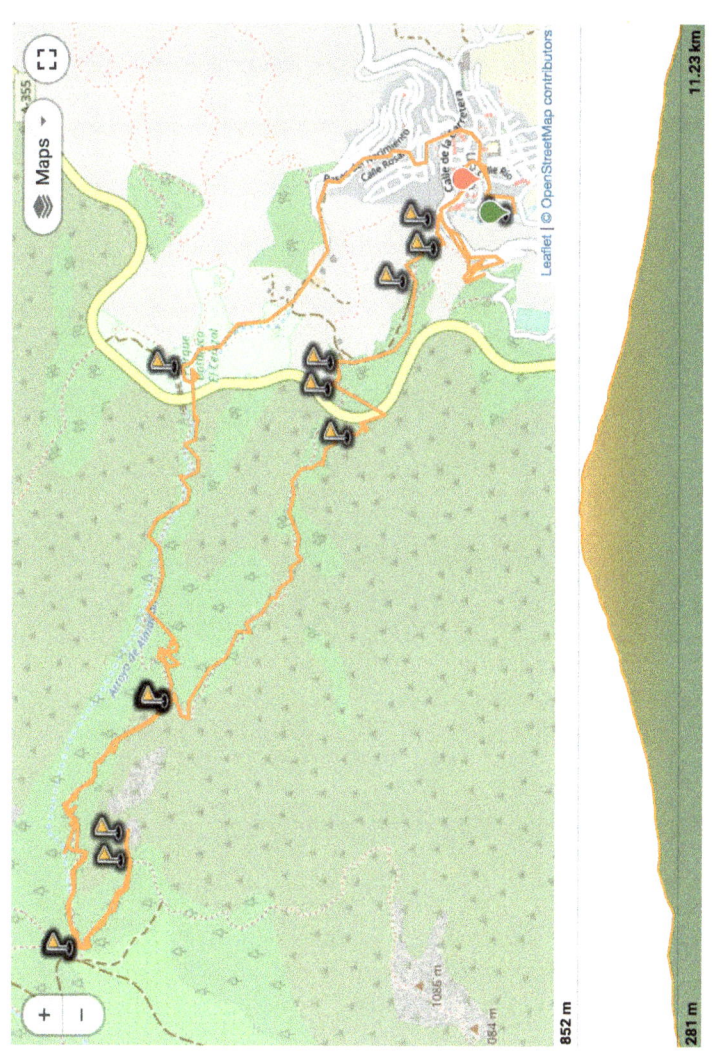

2.2. Monda

Natural beauty

Monda is situated on a plateau at 337 metres. From here, your eyes will be treated to splendid far-reaching views stretching from the Sierra Nevada in the far distance to Torrecilla at 1,919 metres, making it the highest peak of the Serrania de Ronda. In this area, the top of the Sierra Blanca mountain is known as the Sierra de Canucha, which includes the beautiful rugged massif of Los Cuchillos ('The Knives'). Most of the landscape around Monda is mainly dominated by oak, olive, and almond trees. In spring, Monda is an absolute treasure with hundreds of almond trees in full blossom set against the backdrop of grass-green hills and, in the far distance, the snow-capped mountains of the Sierra Nevada

Al-Mundat Castle

From far away, you can see the unusual profile of the Al-Mundat Castle, which is perched on a hilltop in the middle of town. It was initially built by the Muslim ruler Omar Ben Hafsun in the 9th century as a fortress of defence against the Cordobese caliphate. In 1485, he handed it over to the captain of the Catholic Kings, Hurtado de Luna. However, not much later, a Moorish uprising almost completely demolished the castle apart from a tower and parts of the foundations. Since then, it has undergone intensive renovations until reaching its current splendour as a luxury hotel resort.

Caesar's decisive battle

According to legend, the Battle of Munda in 45 B.C. was the final battle of Julius Caesar in a civil war he was leading against the conservative 'Optimates', who formed the opposition party. Thanks to the military victory at Munda, Caesar was able to proudly return in triumph to Rome as governor. It didn't last long, as he was assassinated 1 year later. Monda is one of the regions that like to lay claim to this important battle in Roman history, but it has never been historically proven.

And more…

This small village of about 2,700 inhabitants is famous in the region for more than just its castle. It not only hosts the respected Marbella Design Academy, but also a small olive farm that produces the exquisite Mudéjar brand, which is sold in luxury hotels along the coast. Other points of interest are the tiny 15th-century Santiago Apostle church, the abundance of fountains and crosses, and the Calzada Romana, a tiny Roman road, which is about 700 metres from the village in the direction of Coin.

WALK 16: VIEWPOINTS AT THE HOLY CAVE AND LA CANUCHA

The Facts

Type:	Linear
Length:	13 kilometres
Level:	Moderate
Elevation gain:	572 metres
Time:	3.5 hours return

What to expect

This walk is a one-way climb from Monda castle to the hills and cliff of La Canucha, which is on the Monda side of the Sierra Blanca mountain. Your final destination could be the Cueva Santa (Holy Cave) or, further up, the 360-degree panoramic viewpoint. Initially, the walk runs between farm houses from the castle on the old road to Istán. After a river, the walk becomes more intense as it winds up the hills on a dirt road overgrown with grass. There are only low bushes, so you are completely exposed to the sun at all times. Your effort will be rewarded with spectacular viewpoints of the surrounding mountain ranges up to Torrecilla and even the snow-capped Sierra Nevada in the far distance (in winter). The entrance to the Monda cave is full of small pictures of saints, sculptures, and items put there by locals, pilgrims, and tourists. You can also jot down your personal comments in the book provided. Here, we just explore the entrance to the cave with extreme care and leave the deeper darker area to professional speleologists. The townhall requests visitors not to touch the stalagmites or stalactites as you can damage the growth process that takes hundreds of thousands of years. After the Cueva Santa, there are two options: return or continue up until the views open up on all sides at the end of the road. At that point, experts can choose to climb a more dangerous part next to a deep fall and climb some rocks.

Finish off this Holy Cave experience with a visit to the picturesque church in the village before or after a delicious lunch at the panoramic terrace of the Monda castle. If you liked the olive oil, walk to the Mudéjar olive oil Mill just after the small village centre and take home some unique healthy Extra Virgin Olive Oil.

History, legends and more

Natural and holy caves

There are many natural caves to be found in the region thanks to the geological structure of the karstic limestone mountain with its summits, ravines, and caves that were formed over time by water erosion. These caves were used as shelters by herdsmen and their livestock, as well as places of protection during periods of war. It is believed that the Monda Holy Cave was inhabited by prehistoric people, although there are no cave paintings to confirm this. However, they are not uncommon in other caves in Andalucía. Today, the cave is a place for contemplation, hiking, or speleology. The little relics, María statues, and flowers that are regularly left behind are symbols of the strength and presence of the Christian religion in the minds and traditions of the Andalusian people. Apart from the famous processions during Semana Santa (Easter Week) and the many Saints' holidays throughout the year, their profound beliefs are clearly expressed in many ways. Such offerings can be found in the most unexpected places in Andalucía and throughout Spain, including in natural settings such as caves.

Step-by-step walking guide

- The walk starts at the entrance of the Monda castle. Make your way down on the right side of the castle in the direction of the village centre and school.

- At the bottom of the ramp, walk straight into Calle Istán, which leads you out of the village centre on an ascending country road. You walk between farmhouses with olive and orange trees and lots of barking dogs, which are luckily behind fences.

- At the end of this road, there is a chicken farm where you need to turn right. The dirt road gradually goes up and down and curves around the hill, leaving the village behind.

- Turn left at the signposted rocky trail that zigzags down until the river 'Rio Seco' in the valley. Have a look at the landscape: there's the Sierra Blanca in front, Moratán and Gaimón hills on the right, and, higher up, the Sierra de las Nieves with the Torrecilla peak.

- After crossing the river, the path goes up a few metres and comes to a crossing where there are signposts to Istán and Ojén.

- Cross the street and continue straight upwards. The walk continues on a wide country road that is partly overgrown with grass higher up. This part is the longest and most intense as it climbs the hill slope towards La Canucha on the Sierra Blanca mountain. As the vegetation is low, there are views on the valley on your left.

- At the next turn, keep right, and then a little further on, go left. You come across a small fountain at a stream called the Arroyo Cañada Canucha.

- Behind a bend, the views open up to the valley with the Monda quarry. At the next turn, you must watch out on the left for a wooden signpost with directions to the Cueva Santa.

- Turn onto the Cueva Santa path, which is narrow and rocky. But after only 60 metres of zigzagging up, you arrive at the cave and viewpoint. The cave is right on the top of the Sierra Blanca massive (La Canucha), where you can enjoy far-reaching views of the entire Sierra de las Nieves, including its highest peak of Torrecilla.

- Trace your steps back to the wider dirt road you came from and keep going up to enjoy more wonderful views to la Canucha on the Sierra Blanca and a panoramic 360-degree view. The end of the road is now more overgrown with scrub, but you can continue on the rocks on the left to another natural viewpoint. **IMPORTANT!** This part is dangerous and should only be done by experts and at their own risk, as it runs along a very deep ravine.

- After taking in all the views, go back down to the castle on the same path. The Mudéjar olive oil Mill and shop can be found on the A-7101 road, which leaves the village to the right of the Los Carboneros statue in the Plaza de la Ermita. Opposite the oil mill, just off the road, have a look at the remains of the Calzada Romana (the tiny Roman road).

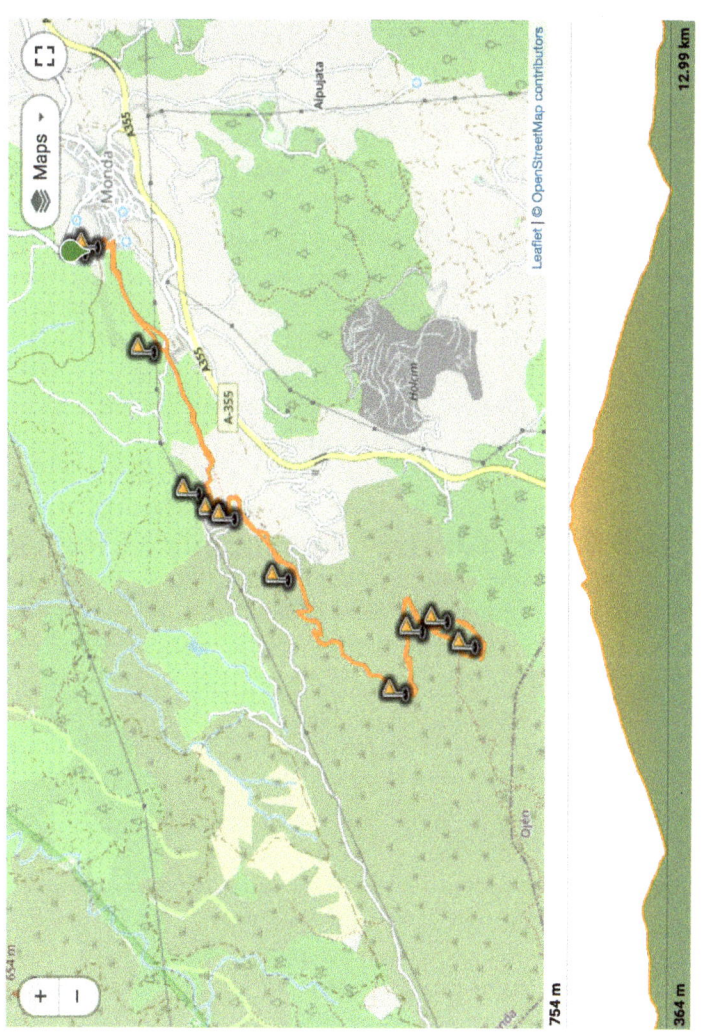

2.3. Istán: important water source for the coast

Green garden of the coast

Istán is the untouched pearl of the Sierra de las Nieves mountain villages. It's located on a cliff at 303 metres next to a spectacular immense reservoir (214 ha) called La Concepción. The reservoir lies on the Rio Verde water-course, which collects water from the mountains and flows into the sea east of Puerto Banus. This tiny village has big treasures; apart from the magnificent man-made lake, it is set between a variety of beautiful mountain ranges. To the west lies the Sierra Real, which has a reddish colour similar to that of the Sierra Bermeja of Estepona. The mountain tops of the Sierra Bermeja are also visible in the distance looking from Istán. Both mountains meet the Serrania de Ronda further away. To the east are the stunning cone-shaped grey limestone peaks of the Sierra Blanca mountain, and to the north is the Sierra de las Nieves. Despite only being a stone's throw away from Marbella (a mere 20-minute drive), it has been able to maintain a low cost of living, which makes the village appealing to elderly people and families with younger children. The community of around 1,500 residents is blessed by nature, fertile soil, and a tranquil lifestyle with the coast just a bus stop away. In recent years, the village has undergone some renovations. The town hall has had a makeover and, after long being abandoned, the rural hotel Los Altos is being refurbished.

Water, water, water

Water originally attracted the Moors to settle here and it has been cleverly exploited by all the people who have lived in this area. It should come as no surprise that Istán received the name '**green garden of the coast**', because its abundance of water is indispensable to the entire coastal area, which often endures droughts. There are long rivers, of which the Rio Verde is the most important, and crashing waterfalls which all originate in the mountains nearby.

The construction of the beautiful 'Pantano de la Concepción' dam in 1971 was the long-awaited answer to the water-supply problems on the western side of the Costa del Sol. The water level is carefully watched and the alarm is raised if it is too low. However, the water is released into the sea if it has reached its capacity after frequent rains.

Water is omnipresent in the centre of Istán village, where you can hear the flow of water rushing through channels under the pavements. These irrigation channels or 'acequias moriscas' were built by the Moors for household use and agriculture. The most outstanding water feature is the Chorro fountain and washing basin with its decorated ceramic tiles in the centre of the village. Its source is the nearby Molinos river, which can be reached by foot from the centre.

The name of the Molinos river refers to the many 'molinos' (mills), which were widespread at the start of the 20th century. These were very productive for grinding corn and wheat grain and served the entire area and the coast.

The Rio Verde that flows into the reservoir has a few 'charcos' (fresh-water pools), where residents love to bathe on hot summer days without having to drive to the coast. The most popular ones are the Charco La Huerta, Charco El Cojo, and El Charco el Cancho, which can get as deep as 4 metres. You can find more information on the water history of Istán in the small Water Museum and the Mill Museum, which are both in the lower part of the village close to the cemetery.

Panochos

The people of Istán are called 'panochos', from a tradition dating back to the first Christians who moved here in an effort to Christianize the Moorish village. They came from the countryside of Murcia, where a dialect called 'pinocho' was spoken.

Hikers and bikers delight

Istán is extremely popular among hikers and cyclists. Day tourists are part of everyday life and on a typical day the village may well have more than 100 cyclists making the 12-kilometre climb to Istán from Marbella. Another popular long route for mountain bikers is the dirt road up to the famous and enormous 800-year-old chestnut tree called 'el Castaño Santo' (the Sacred Chestnut Tree).

WALK 17: ISTÁNS'MAGIC RESERVOIR AND CHAPEL: CAMINO DE LA CUESTA

The Facts

Type:	Circular
Length:	5.86 kilometres
Level:	Moderate
Elevation gain:	270 metres
Time:	2 hours 20 min

What to expect

You can't get closer to the reservoir than on the 'Camino de la Cuesta' or 'Hill Walk' (the PR-A137). This path passes through the lower part of the village and runs by the water's edge, giving onto the best views of the reservoir's calm waters and its beautiful natural setting looking towards the Sierra Palmitera on the other side. On your return, you'll pass by the cave chapel of San Miguel (St. Michael), who is the patron saint of Istán. Nearby, there is a picnic and barbecue area.

This walk mainly runs on easy wide dirt roads (some parts are on older tarmac roads) and is very well signposted. However, there is one small part where you must be careful: it's right at the start, close to the reservoir. The path is narrow, uneven with holes, and partly runs between dense vegetation and partly next to the steep slopes by the reservoir. After about 100 metres, it opens up and continues on an easy, gradually ascending, wider dirt road. This shorter but trickier part may not be appropriate for anyone with a fear of heights.

History, stories and more

Rio Verde reservoir

The reservoir is also called Rio Verde as it was built on a 5-kilometre stretch of the river. The greenish colour of the water is caused by algae that clean and purify the water. The lake is the habitat of otters, which are quite rare to find in Málaga.

Archangel San Miguel

San Miguel (St. Michael), the patron saint of Istán, protects the inhabitants from his protected white cave hermitage at the entrance of the village. As the chief angel of God's army, he blows the trumpet on Judgement Day and faces the devil to protect the people. The beautiful sculpture represents him as a warrior angel threatening Lucifer with a spear. Once a year, he is taken out and carried around the village in the Tomillería procession. This reflects the tradition of pilgrimages in earlier days, when a donkey was still used to reach the chapel. The pilgrimage derives its name from 'tomillo' (thyme) to refer to the huge amounts that grow in the area. The church in the main square, also named after San Miguel, dates back to the 16th century.

Step-by-step walking guide

- At the entrance to the village, take the second street on the right to make your way up to the public parking area. The walk starts here in the car park on the Plaza de Calvario.

- Walk down into the village on Calle Calvario, passing the Chorro fountain.

- At the plaza del Pueblo, go into Calle Rio, which is the first narrow descending street on the left before the church. Continue by the white wall until the junction where you can admire fabulous mountain views.

- Go left at the information board and follow the old steeply descending tarmac street. You quickly leave the village behind as you move on towards the valley and reservoir. Now there are no more houses, barking dogs, or farms.

- The paved road changes into a dirt path with lots of holes and bumps, especially at the lower end. The path zigzags down to the tail end of the reservoir, which is a great spot for a photo shoot.

- With the reservoir in front, take a very sharp left onto the narrow stretch that now follows. There is a signpost warning of the ravine next to the path. This narrow path runs along the rock cliff for a few metres and can at times be overgrown with plants. However, it quickly opens up again becoming an easy accessible (although still narrow) path parallel to the waters' edge.

- You'll be rewarded for completing this more challenging part by beautiful views over the reservoir or, after a dry season, towards the green meadows that recall the earlier Rio Verde valley before the dam was built.

- The next part gradually goes up on a wide footpath, away from the water, and meanders through the mountains. Keep the valley to your right. At the turns, always stay on the left of the path, which is well signposted all along the way.

- Reach the Istán road, cross it, and walk towards the Ermita de San Miguel parking area. On the left side there is a path with a wooden balustrade which zigzags up to the small white St. Michael chapel. It's built in a cave and has a fabulous viewpoint to the lake and the mountain ranges of the Sierra Bermeja (left), Sierra Palmitera (middle), and Sierra Real (right).

- Walk along the dirt road until the end.

- Turn left on a tarmac road. After passing some country houses, you arrive in the upper part of the village. You'll come across the Hotel los Altos with its view of the impressive grey cone-shaped peak 'El Picacho' in the Sierra Blanca.

- Pass the hotel and the sportsfield and go down to the village parking area. But first, take a look at the Moorish irrigation channels in the valley on your right.

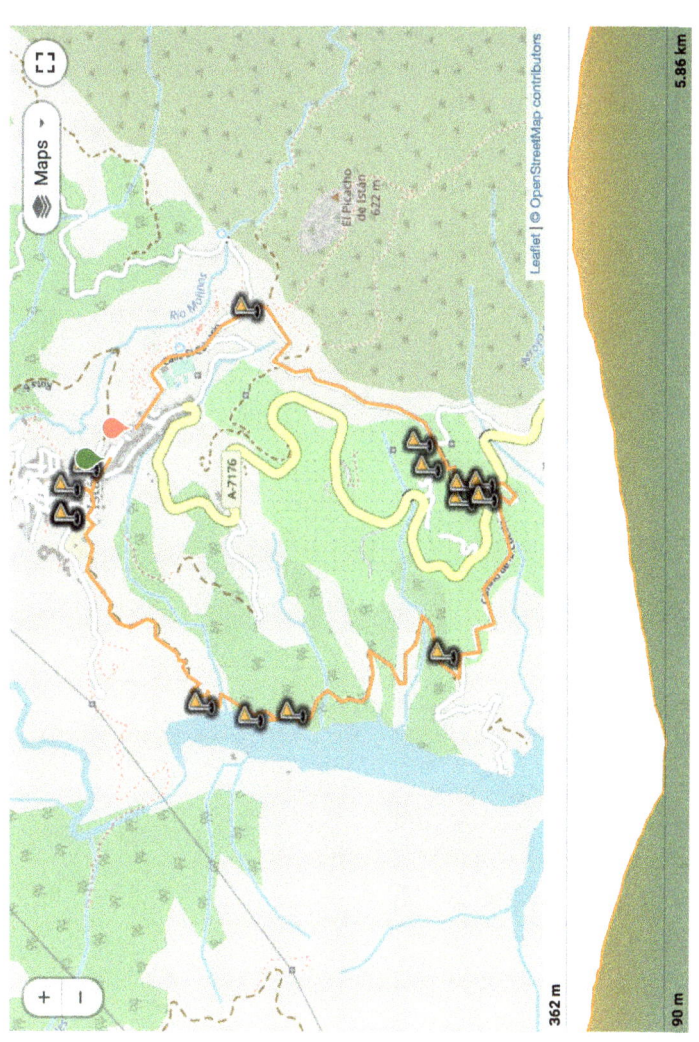

WALK 18: SPECTACULAR VIEWPOINTS OF ISTÁN

The facts

Type:	Circular
Length:	5 kilometres
Level:	Easy
Elevation:	200 metres
Time:	1.5 hours

What to expect

Take in all the best viewpoints of Istán on this circular walk around the village. After an initial visit to the breathtaking viewpoints of el Tajo Banderas and Herriza at the reservoir, the walk continues on the official itinerary of 'Herrizas de la Gallega', indicated as the PR-A 166. The sound of water is your companion for most of this walk, which runs over the fertile land in the Rio Molinos valley. Having reached the hill on the opposite side, you can admire the village from a distance. From here you can see how it was courageously built on high rock formations, which you may not have noticed if you have arrived from the coast.

This walk shows you the true characteristics of Istán with its water features, small farming plots, and land which was hard to cultivate or build on. This is what the word 'herriza' refers to: a stony piece of land on a hill which can't be effectively exploited.

From this side, you can very much appreciate the different mountains in the region, with Istán connecting the greyish Sierra Blanca and the green-red Sierra de las Nieves mountain ranges. The path is easy to follow, although some parts are narrower. You must take extra care at these points because of some steep drops.

History, stories and more

Tajo Banderas Viewpoint

This is not about Antonio Banderas! The name refers to the different wars that were fought in the area and the opponents' 'banderas' (flags) that were raised on this spot. From this paved viewpoint, enjoy the views towards Istán with its backdrop of the Sierra Blanca mountains with La Concha, El Picacho, and Tajo Bermejo marking the horizon.

Herriza II Viewpoint

From here, there are gorgeous displays of colours and views over the entire reservoir and the very different mountains on either side of it. To the east is the greyish-green limestone of the Sierra Blanca mountain and to the west the reddish colour of the formerly volcanic Sierra Bermeja, Sierra Palmitera, and Sierra Real. To the north are the green fir forests on the Sierra de las Nieves. And in the middle, there is the vibrant green and blue of the Rio Verde.

El Peñon Viewpoint

In front of you is the Sierra Real, at whose foot the Rio Verde flows bordered by a lush forest of oak trees. On the higher slopes grows the rare fir tree or 'pinsapo', which is emblematic of this red-coloured mountain.

Step-by-step walking guide

- Start at the Plaza de Pueblo behind San Miguel church, passing its side entrance, to make your way down the Calle Rio road. At the junction, pass the cemetery, where the starting points for some of the walks are indicated.

- Go left and continue to the end, where you can enjoy the Tajo de Banderas and Herriza viewpoints with views to the village and reservoir. Trace your steps back to the cemetery and continue straight on until the end, where the el Peñon viewpoint is at the end of the Calle Pablo Picasso. Retrace your steps on the same street and go sharp right where you can find the path at a junction with a sudden steep drop. You mustn't get distracted when driving these small precipitous roads at night!

- The old tarmac road on your right goes down steeply but not for long.

- Turn sharp left at the bottom and walk down the hill staying on this country road. On the way, you come across a small mill that was once the driving force behind the local economy.

- The road ends at the entrance gate to a property. On the right, the walk continues on a narrow steep path that zigzags up the hill. Then, almost unexpectedly, it gives onto a wider tarmac platform which offers an excellent viewpoint towards the village.

- The walk continues to the right on a wide country road, known among the locals as the 'La Gallega'. Green avocado trees accompany you until you cross a small stream.

- Further down the path there is a small wooden bridge at the base of an impressive rock. Here and there you'll meet an old farmer working his vegetable garden and not at all put off by having to walk up and down the paths.
- Behind the rock, the path ends at the old tarmac road, where you turn right to soon close the circuit and return to the village on this last climb up.

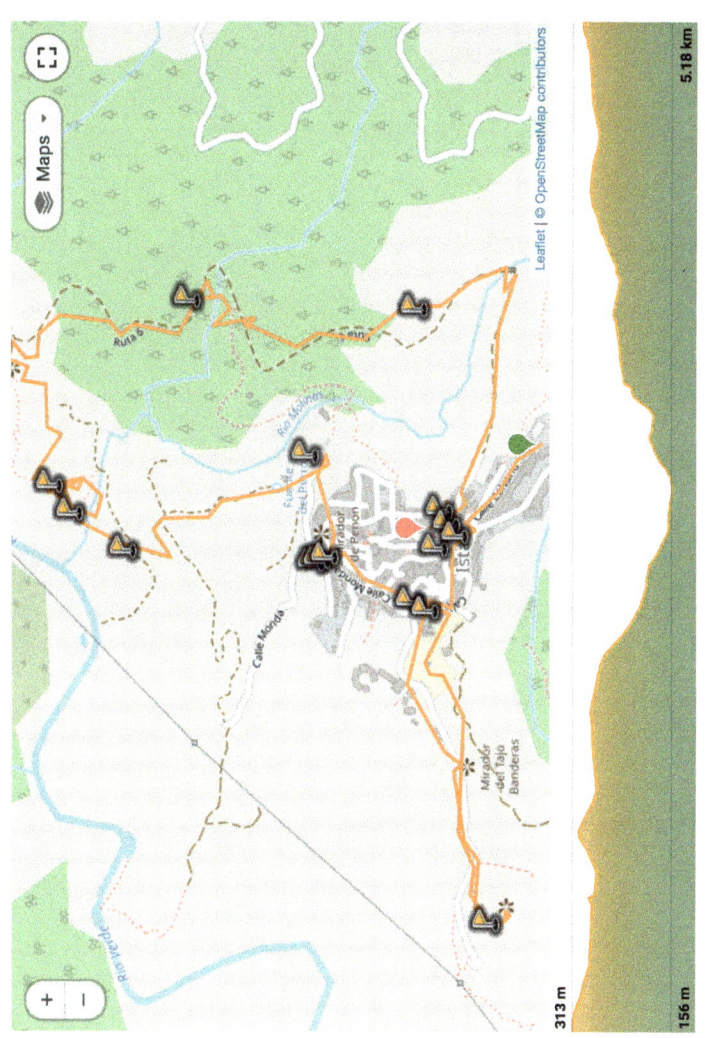

WALK 19: WATER FUN AT THE ROCK POOLS OF THE CHARCO DEL CANALÓN

The Facts

Type:	Linear
Length:	5 kilometres return
Level:	Easy
Elevation gain:	170 metres
Time:	1.5 hours return

What to expect

This walk takes you to the paradise of crystal clear mountain water, small waterfalls, and rock pools of the Rio Verde Valley and the Charco del Canalón. There are two ways to experiencing this walk: dry or wet. You start from the river at Vado de Bornoque, where you must choose between walking on a country dirt road through forest hills until reaching the Charco del Canalón or make your way through the river, which can be deep and slippery. If you are up for the latter, make sure you are fit enough to swim because some parts can be deep and other parts lie between high rocks with nothing to hold on to. We take the less adventurous option, where we need to cross the shallows of the river twice. The path is well signposted from the start all the way to the waterfall. Although the walk runs parallel to the river, which you have to cross, you don't see it: but you do hear the power of the river flow. On the way back, there are some beautiful views towards Istán village with the Sierra Blanca mountain on the left. Allow for some additional time to relax, dip in the water, and admire the beautiful waterfall of which Istán is proud. Although you can walk the entire 7 kilometres from the village, you can shorten it by driving closer. But the walk wouldn't be so special: after all, the objective is to enjoy the river, waterfalls, and pools.

History, stories and more

Charco del Canalón

The Charco del Canalón is a long narrow deep pool in the Rio Verde that lies in a small gorge of limestone rock faces. The name is said come from the water falling from an irrigation system slightly above it. At the further end of the Charco, the rock pools are shallow and safer to have a dip in. The Rio Verde has lots of algae, which turn the water green and make the rocks slippery to walk on. The river banks are covered with abundant cork oaks, pine trees, junipers, heather, and more.

Driving directions

About 20 minutes drive from Marbella, arrive in Istán, and take the very first road to the right towards the Hotel los Altos. From this point, it is another 20-minute drive down the hills behind the village. Cross the road, opposite the football pitch, and take the asphalted road in the direction of Monda for about 3 kilometres. At the first turn, you'll pass the Rio Molinos source at a beautiful rock. The asphalted road turns into a dirt road, still going in the direction of Monda. Continue zigzagging down and at the turn, keep left. The road is cut by the river and just before it there is a parking area at Vado de Bornoque.

Step-by-step walking guide

- From the car park, walk down a few metres towards the river, cross it, and turn immediately right to walk uphill. However, the larger stream can be found just a few metres further straight ahead on this same road (before going uphill). Keep this in mind, because you might want to refresh yourself with a dip after the walk.

- If the gate on the road is closed, take the more enjoyable small hill path on the left to pass it. The path to the Charco mainly runs on private land, but it has official signposts and access is permitted.

- Follow the dirt road upwards and keep right at a fork.

- After crossing the Almedinilla river, the path will gradually start to go down.

- You'll pass some country houses at La Palomera. Keep right on the same dirt road, which curves around the mountain in the area of Vega Pedrizas.

- Cross the Rio Verde river and continue for 10 metres uphill. If the river is too high, the townhall suggests you finish your walk here (we have never seen it higher than at our ankles). You can see a hanging bridge over it, but it is completely broken. At the next turn, there's a path that takes you to  the waterfall just a few metres further along. It runs through the forest and you have to walk over some big rocks.

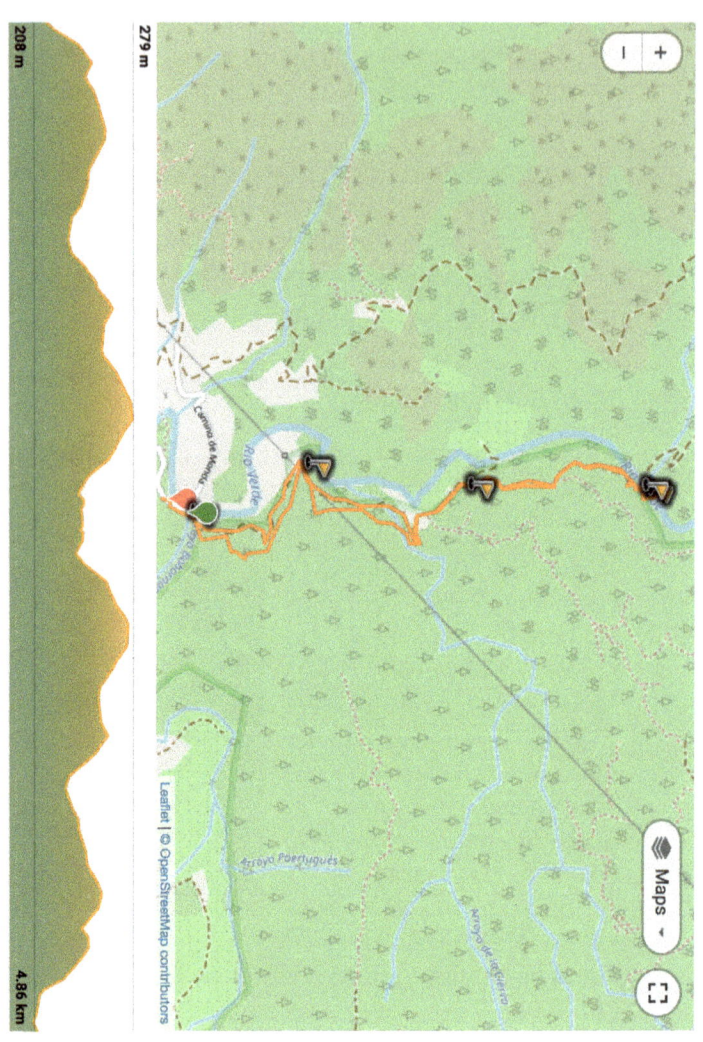

Tips

'The best of' walk: See the best of Istán in one walk by extending it to about 11 kilometres. Just combine the reservoir and viewpoints walks described above, as they both connect up in the church square.

The 'Waterfall' walk: A walk to the beautiful waterfall of the Charco del Canalón is possible from the village, but it is a linear and less exciting walk.

The 'Old Istán-Marbella path' walk: This walk is described under Marbella Walks because the path runs on the Sierra Blanca mountain. It can be done in reverse, starting from the village of Istán.

There are some more difficult walks for experienced hikers and climbers, including the route up to La Concha. All of these start from the part above Hotel Los Altos.

2.4. Benahavis: a gastronomic gem in the mountains

If you want to finish off a walk in nature with some tasty local dishes afterwards, Benahavis is a place not to be missed. This charming white village is set within beautifully preserved natural surroundings on the lower slopes of the large mountain range of the Sierra Bermeja. A mere 7-kilometre drive from the beaches of Marbella and Estepona, Benahavis can be quite busy with tourists in the high season, but it's very authentic and peaceful with a very close community of locals during the rest of the year.

The main access road takes you there in no time. It zigzags gently between the sunny hills becoming narrower by the Guadalmina river, which has cut a dramatic and beautiful canyon. Here, the more adventurous visitors like to go climbing and swimming, especially in the warm summer months.

After passing the canyon and a bend, you suddenly come to a beautiful roundabout with a tower fountain. This is the beginning of the municipality of Benahavis with all of its typical Andalusian features: white town-houses, steep winding streets, a little church, and the ruin of a Moorish castle. However, in contrast to many other villages, it is neither the church nor the castle that first strike the eyes. Its strongest appeal lies in the natural settings, the top-notch restaurants, and the well-tended facilities, including playgrounds, a wide range of sports fields, and wooden footpaths. You may even bump into an international football team training there.

Glorious food

Benahavis proudly hosts a catering school that has contributed to the village's reputation as a gastronomic gem. It bursts with excellent restaurants staffed by highly trained professional waiters and chefs who miraculously prepare the most exquisite meals in tiny kitchens.

Loved by all

The region has attracted artists including David Marshall,

whose art sculptures and works can be found in the gallery bearing his name. He's not the only foreigner who has fallen in love with Benahavis. Over the years, many British people have settled here, trying to smoothly blend in with the local community. Fortunately, the village remains Spanish in soul and character with crowded loud local bars during the typical Spanish morning break. The rising demand of expats to have a place in the sun here has again inspired builders, and contemporary projects are slowly changing the landscape of the village.

Natural heritage

Typical to these mountainous regions, the sunny hills around the village are densely covered with plants and trees including shrubs, pines, chestnuts, and olive trees. The geology is very rich and includes marble and granite. The rivers emerging in

the Serrania de Ronda—the Guadalmina, Guadalmansa, and Guadaiza—criss-cross each other here and flow down to the Mediterranean Sea.

There are also lots of wild animals, including mountain goats, deer, reptiles, and wild boar. Their tracks can be found almost everywhere, but the animals are shy so you rarely get to spot them.

A little dip into history

The name Benahavis was given to the village during the Moorish period. The true origin of its name is hard to trace, but there are a few interesting stories. 'Ben' could come from 'son of' and 'Havis' could refer to the name of the ruler of the Montemayor castle. It may also be derived from Ben Habix, a family that may have settled here. Other names also evoke this part of history, like 'guad', which is Arabic for 'river'. Guadalmina was named after the neighbouring mines, Guadalmansa refers to 'almazara' or olive oil press, and Guadalaiza comes from the Sultana Aixa. She was the politically active mother of Boabdil, the last Emir of Granada, who did everything in her power to save the city. When King Ferdinand took possession of Marbella in 1485, he was also handed the keys to other areas in the region including Benahavis. It would take until 1572 before the municipality was granted independence by King Philip II.

Walk 20: Benahavis lake, mountain and Montemayor castle

The Facts

Type:	Circular
Level:	Moderate
Length:	10.3 kilometres(11.38 km inc castle)
Elevation gain:	463 metres (489 m inc castle)
Time:	3 hours (4 hours inc castle)

What to expect

There are two well-signposted hiking trails around the village, the Sendero de las Libélulas (the Dragonflies' walk) and the walk up to the ruins of Montemayor. The route suggested here makes a nice big loop into the mountains on the west side of the village and includes both these short walks. So, carefully follow the instructions given here, as this walk deviates from the marked paths. The walk starts from the lower part of the village on a path next to the river, loops around the beautiful lake, then goes up the mountain on a dirt road. It runs over the hill with views opening up on the other side looking towards Estepona and far-off Gibraltar. It starts to go down next to a higher hill on which the castle is located (at 579 m). The itinerary mainly runs along easy ascending wider paths except for this extra linear stretch that goes up to the castle. If you do this part, you should add an additional hour. This part of the walk is narrow and uphill with a deep fall to one side, and so it is not recommended after rainy days or if you have a fear of heights. This linear stretch deviates from the circular walk, so it is up to you if you want to hike it or skip it.

History, stories and more

Dragonflies

In Benahavis, between May and September, some 28 types of dragonflies can be spotted here. Three of them are of African origin and have likely arrived due to the influence of climate change.

Guadalmina reservoir

The Guadalmina dam is a bypass dam that transports water from the eponymous river through a 9.5-kilometre tunnel to the Rio Verde dam in Istán.

Montemayor

The castle of Montemayor was erected in the 10th century and was long an important defence point where many battles took place. The only well-preserved parts are the Tower of the Queen, which features several rooms. The fortified complex also included a set of watchtowers. It is easy to imagine the strategic perfection of the Montemayor castle, with views stretching over 100 kilometres of coastline and all the way to Africa.

Later, the site served as a hiding place for the resistance during the Napoleonic Wars.

Step-by-step walking guide

- The route starts on the left behind the village's well-maintained football pitch, at the Sendero de las Libélulas. Unless it is a very dry season, you can usually enjoy the rippling river by which this footpath initially runs.

- After the first turn, go left and walk towards the dam on a short uphill tarmac road, leaving the dam on your left. The views open up towards the Guadalmina reservoir and the hills that surround it. Walk straight towards the lakeside.

- Then go down left and continue towards the lake, which you have to cross. There's always a handful of peaceful ducks and swans swimming on the water, so keep an eye on your dog if it's off the leash.

- On the other side of the lake, go right, thus ignoring the signpost to the left, which would take you straight back to the higher part of the village. Walk straight through the gate into the pine forest and keep left going up a broad unpaved road.

- At a turn, after a farmer's house, go straight ahead and then pay attention at the T-junction; turn left, even though there's a signpost pointing to the right.

- Now continue uphill for a bit and go left at a V-junction.

- At the next fork, keep left going uphill until you walk out of the denser forest, where magnificent views slowly come into view. Continue towards the huge antenna on the plateau of the dry pale mountain and pass it by.

- Go down to the left, behind the derelict finca (plot), then immediately bear right along the valley, keeping it to your left.

- A bit further along at the next turn, go right uphill. Take a break to admire the surrounding countryside with views over the forests and the village all the way to the housing project behind it.

- At the top you come to a small plateau with large pine trees. Angle left to start going down the gentle slope along the valley on your right. There are views reaching as far as the Rock of Gibraltar. If you carefully look ahead, you can spot the Moorish ruin on the mountain top.

- Continue walking alongside the fence of a private property. The unpaved road ends at the entrance gate to it. You can now choose to either go down on your immediate left to the asphalt road to the village or take a very worthwhile short detour to the castle ruins. This follows a narrow steep path with a deep fall by it. If you include this part of the walk, you have to allow another extra hour, there and back.

- The asphalted road takes you back down to the village, but first passes a hotel with a residential area.

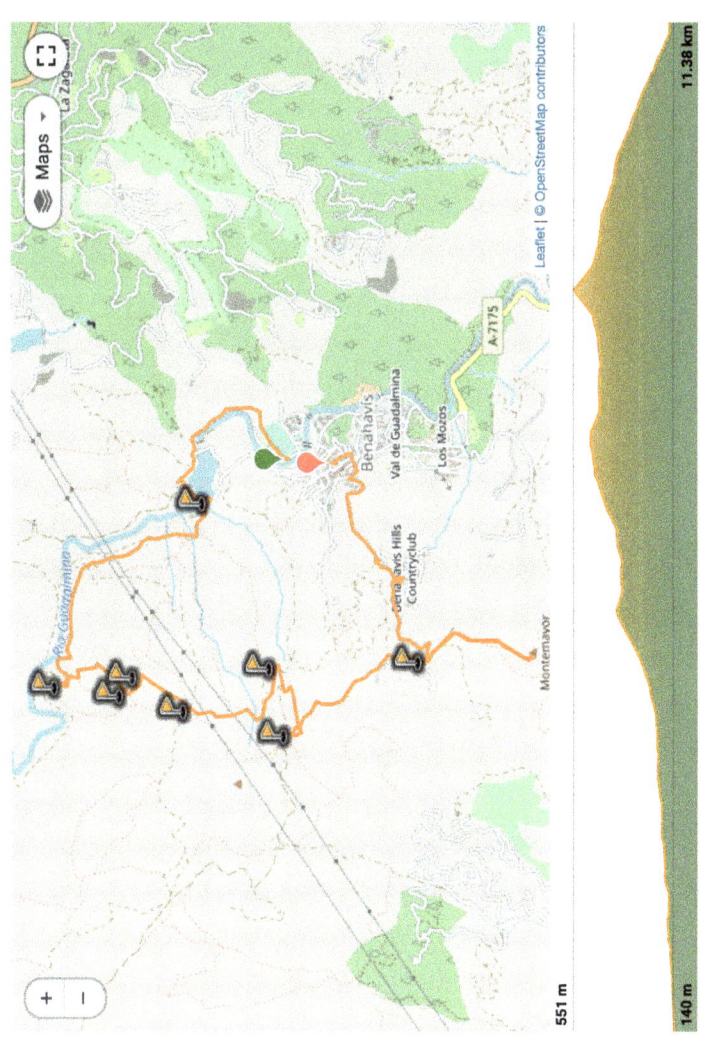

Walk 21: Benahavis: Arab irrigation channels and river walk

The Facts

Type:	Circular, partly linear
Level:	Easy
Length:	7.7 kilometres
Elevation gain:	104 metres
Time:	1.5 hours

What to expect

Experience a pleasant easy walk above refreshing water irrigation channels at the end of the Guadalmina river in a natural setting of green hills and rocks. Adjacent to the channel are little information boards on the plants to be found in the area, such as the Acebuche or wild olive tree. The walk is a circuit that follows the course of the river, which you cross using a wooden suspension bridge above the Angosturas canyon. The path has recently been made longer with an exciting part on a narrow path with wooden handrails that runs along the grey limestone cliff walls of the canyon. Caution is the watchword here because there are falling rocks. This path takes you to another irrigation channel and viewpoint looking towards the El Higueral golf course. The path includes a picnic area. In summer, you can end your walk with a refreshing dip in the Charco de las Mozas pool. Your dog will equally enjoy this trail above and along the river, as it follows some water-filled irrigation channels. Along the route, there are also some small information boards on plants and trees. Splash along and learn.

History, stories and more

Acequias

The acequias (water channels) were a clever invention by the Moors, who built them more than 10 centuries ago to irrigate the surrounding farmlands and provide houses with water from the Guadalmina river. The system used the topography of the land to move water around, a brilliantly simple principle still in use today. The current channels were built on top of the old ones and then metal walkways were placed on top of them to make access easier and more enjoyable .

Walk versus adventure

From a safe distance, watch the more adventurous tourists swim their way through the canyon below you. In summer, this gets pretty interesting. There's a contrast between the relaxed tourists in their bathing suits and organized canyoning clubs equipped with lifejackets, helmets, and wetsuits. The latter are clearly better prepared for the challenge of canyoning, which also includes the risk of falling rocks. As yet, there are no rules and regulations on this activity, but maybe there'll be some 'mañana'!

Driving directions

On the A-7 going towards Algeciras, take the Benahavis exit. About 2 kilometres before the entrance to Benahavis village, you can see a white and blue wall and a car park. Park in the large car park next to the hermitage of Nuestra Señora del Rosario.

Step-by-step walking guide

- From the hermitage, walk beside the road and white wall for about 500 metres until you see the Mirador de las Tres Pergolas. This has wooden benches and a wooden suspension bridge over the Angosturas canyon.

- Cross the bridge and follow a footpath that zigzags upwards until you reach the irrigation channel. The path runs beside this for about 1.2 kilometres. It then turns into a dirt road until it ends at the tarmac road.

- Turn right on the road and cross the bridge.

- The footpath continues down just after the bridge on the right side.
- Go sharp right immediately under the bridge. On this linear part of the walk, the path leads you along by the river, cliffs and water channels for about 3.2 kilometres (return). The El Higueral viewpoint is in the middle of the path and there's a picnic area at the end of the irrigation channels.
- Once back at the bridge, go right. Continue on the path by the lower water channels, where there is a small viewpoint over the river, until you reach the car park.

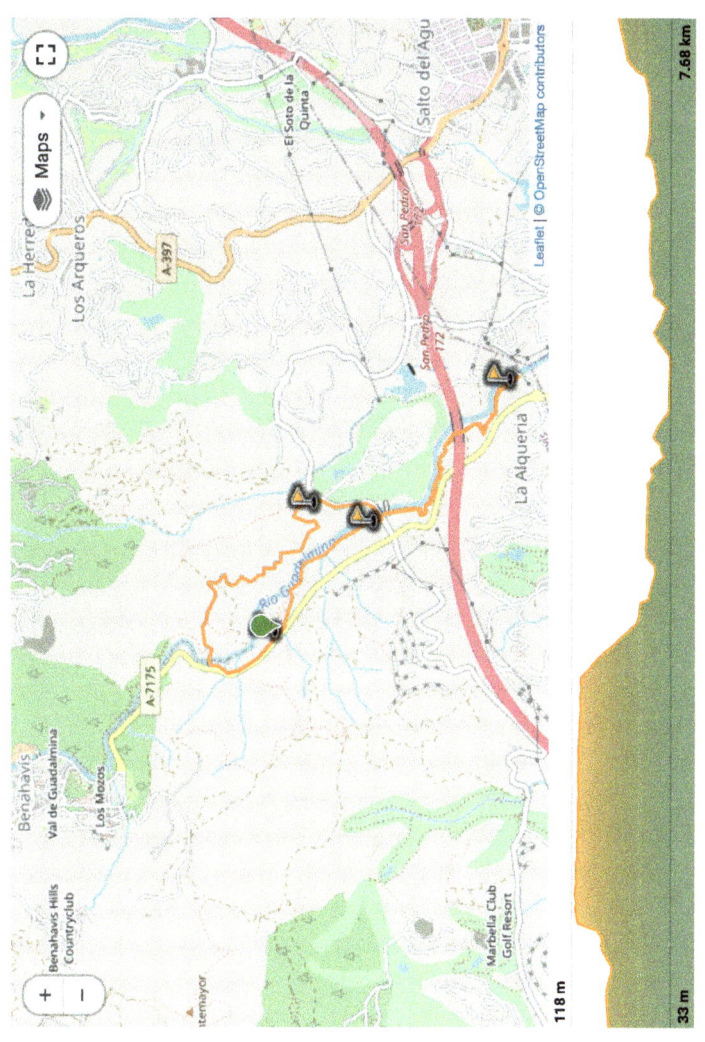

PART 3. Spectacular nature and beautiful sites a little further away

A variety of Natural Parks within reach

Marbella is blessed by the sea, the beaches, the nearby Sierra Blanca and Sierra de las Nieves Natural Park, as well as the foothills of the Serrania de Ronda. Quite a lot to keep you going! But if you are ready to explore a little further, you'll be wowed by the incredible variety of nature you can find within less than 1.5 hours' drive. And the drive is never boring because you cut through mountains and scenic landscapes to get to your walking destination.

To the west, there are the red mountains of the Sierra Bermeja and the cork-tree forests of the Sierra de Alcornocales, a natural park shared between the provinces of Cádiz and Málaga. To the northwest lie the olive groves and chestnut landscapes of the Serrania de Ronda and the grass-green hills of the Sierra Grazalema, another natural park shared with Cádiz. To the east are the dry steep Sierra de Mijas, the magic El Chorro, and the Montes de Málaga. We don't cover the Sierras Tejeda, Almijara, and Alhama, which lie in an area between Málaga and Granada, because they are outside the regions described here. However, all the other natural parks mentioned are very close to each other, just under 2-hours' drive from one another, and yet they are all so different. They offer an unlimited range of walks for every season and taste.

The Desfiladero de los Gaitanes is one of these wonderful natural parks. It is better known as El Chorro and has received international attention with the opening of the Caminito del Rey (King's Path), which runs along a breathtaking gorge. In no time, it rightly reached the top list of excursions for active tourism. However, not many people know yet about the spectacular canyon of the griffon vultures. It's certain that this natural park and other national monuments will soon be put on the list of international travel destinations.

A hike for every season

These mountains are not too far from Marbella, and it's extraordinary to experience the change of seasons in them. In autumn, you have to head to the colourful chestnut hills of the Valle del Genal, where typically quiet villages come alive and get busy collecting chestnuts for international export. It's also the start of the olive harvesting season, when farmers are hard at work on the otherwise deserted olive groves around the Serrania de Ronda. Olives are brought to the nearest fully operating oil mills for pressing and bottling. Some municipalities, such as Monda, have small mills, whereas others, like Ronda, have larger industrial ones. There are abundant olive groves and bodegas (wineries) around Ronda, Acinipo, and Setenil. In winter, the Sierra de las Nieves might surprise you with snow, very cold days, and incredible views to the snowy peaks of the Sierra Nevada in Granada province. Unless it is snowing, it's a perfect time to undertake the longer trek to the peak of this range, La Torrecilla at 1,919 metres. The summits of the Sierra Bermeja and Sierra de Mijas can be magic on a sunny winter day, when the morning fog slowly vanishes to reveal the astonishing views. Spring is absolutely amazing everywhere with colourful flowers and blossoming trees. This is a good time to visit El Torcal, where the temperatures can be very extreme in winter and summer. And in the summer season, it can be very refreshing to walk next to river banks, like those in Benaoján or Cortes de la Frontera, or to stroll by a lake like the one in El Chorro.

A hike for every taste

If you like art and history, check out Ronda or the fascinating art village of Genalguacil. Or immerse yourself in a Spanish tradition and visit Ronda's bullring. For a taste of Roman history, walk around the ruins of Acinipo. Entertain the little ones by visiting the blue-painted village of Juzcár. Give your teenagers a thrilling experience and walk the Caminito del Rey. If you like challenges, hike the mountain summits. Or simply lose yourself in nature by visiting the karst landscape of El Torcal or the Spanish fir woods of the formerly volcanic Sierra Bermeja.

White villages & stories

The villages around these natural parks and places of interest are always worth a visit, as each one has its own story, charm, and architectural settings. And yes, they do look a bit alike, because they were initially created as hamlets by the Moors and adorned with Christian elements and churches by the Catholic rulers after 1485. If you are curious about their secrets, keep an eye open when passing through their narrow streets and read the street names, words written on tiles, and wall inscriptions.

3.1. DIRECTION RONDA & NORTH OF RONDA

WALK 22: SIERRA DE LAS NIEVES: LA TORRECILLA PEAK

If you are an advanced hiker exploring the region between Ronda and Marbella, your sense of adventure will certainly be sparked by the more intense route to the peak of La Torrecilla at 1,919 metres. Together with la Concha (at 1,215 m), they are the most well-known mountain peaks in the region of the Sierra de las Nieves. This is not surprising as you can see both summits from almost everywhere. Torrecilla is a relatively secluded and higher area of the Sierra de las Nieves, in the municipality of Tolox, and has remained relatively untouched. The 'Quejigo' or Portuguese oaks are typical here, but closer to the summit there's only sparse vegetation, leaving the mountain a very special pale grey.

The Facts

Type:	Linear-partly circular
Length:	16.68 kilometres
Level:	Hard
Elevation gain:	742 metres
Time:	6 hours return

What to expect

The walk starts at 1,177 metres and takes you to the peak at 1,919 metres. This is a serious trek, but it mainly runs over easy paths with no technical difficulties or ravines. But take care at the top because there are deep falls there. The walk is very beautiful and your effort will be rewarded with 360-degree far-reaching views all the way to Málaga and the Sierra Nevada, Gibraltar, and the African coast, as well as the surrounding mountain ranges of the Sierra Blanca, Sierra Bermeja, the Genal valley, and the Serrania de Ronda. It can be fun to try to identify the white villages from the summit.

A good attempt has been made to set up walking poles, but you must be very careful not to deviate from the path. Broadly speaking, the route consists of three parts: forest, plateau, and the bald mountain top. After zigzagging up through the oak and pine forest 'Pinsapar de Ronda', you reach the los Pilones plateau. This place looks like you've landed on a moon, with its bare grey limestone landscape with some short vegetation. It may seem far away from the world to you, but it's home to the sheep that cross your path. Finally, in the distance, you'll see the third part of the walk, the hill with its path zigzagging up to the summit. IMPORTANT! Although you can do this walk all year round, watch out for snow in winter. Also, extreme heat and forest fires are not uncommon in July and August.

The adventure really starts with the 10-kilometre drive up to the starting point at the Cortijo de Quejigales. The dirt road to the cortijo is very uneven with deep holes. It curves around the hill with steep slopes on the last stretch. So, just leave the sports car at home! You'll also find yourself driving through the home of immense black bulls wandering across the road with their impressive horns. If you think of this trip as a kind of Spanish safari, being shaken up and down a bit won't seem a big deal.

History, stories and more

Snow wells

On the plateau, the most visible remains of human activity are the large wells dug into the ground. These were the fridges, or snow wells, of the 17th century. They have been restored to show how this resource was used in the mountains when the winters were colder and there was more snow. Until the 20th century, these stone wells were used to make ice by storing and compacting snow in them. The ice was not only used for cooling drinks, but also as an anti-inflammatory. To avoid the sun, the ice was transported to the nearby cities and coast at night. There are many such wells in the Sierra de las Nieves, Sierra Grazalema, and Sierra Tejeda, but only a handful are well conserved.

Driving directions

From San Pedro de Alcántara, take the A-397 towards Ronda, then leave it by going right at kilometre 13, which is just before the big petrol station. Now drive through the Quejigales natural reserve until reaching the Cortijo de los Quijigales 10 kilometres further on. You'll arrive at a car park, where there's an information board about the walk.

Step-by-step walking guide

- After strolling for a few metres along a wide pebble path by a rippling river, you immediately turn right and dive into the forest. The first climb begins here, goes up to a small clearing, and then zigzags upwards. A little higher up, you can see the first views towards Ronda between the trees.

- After about 40 minutes, you come out of the dense pine and oak forest on a relatively visible path. There is only one ambiguous turn, where you have to keep to the right. Follow this to the plateau of los Pilones at 1,690 metres.

- On the plateau, take a left turn until you reach a fork.

- Go right at this fork, where you'll see a signpost to Torrecilla. You are now at 1,729 metres. In the far distance, you can see the snowy tops of the Sierra Nevada. Walk over the rocks around Pilar and head straight towards the top of Torrecilla.

- The path gently zigzags up, mainly on the same side of the mountain. At the top it gets steeper and narrower.

- There's enough room for a group to rest at the summit.

- To return, you can retrace your steps or make a little circuit.

- The circuit: Go back down to where you passed the Torrecilla signpost at the bottom of the hill. Go left instead of right (where you came from). This route will continue on the plateau through the forest in the direction of Puerto de los Pilones, from where you walk down the same way you came up.

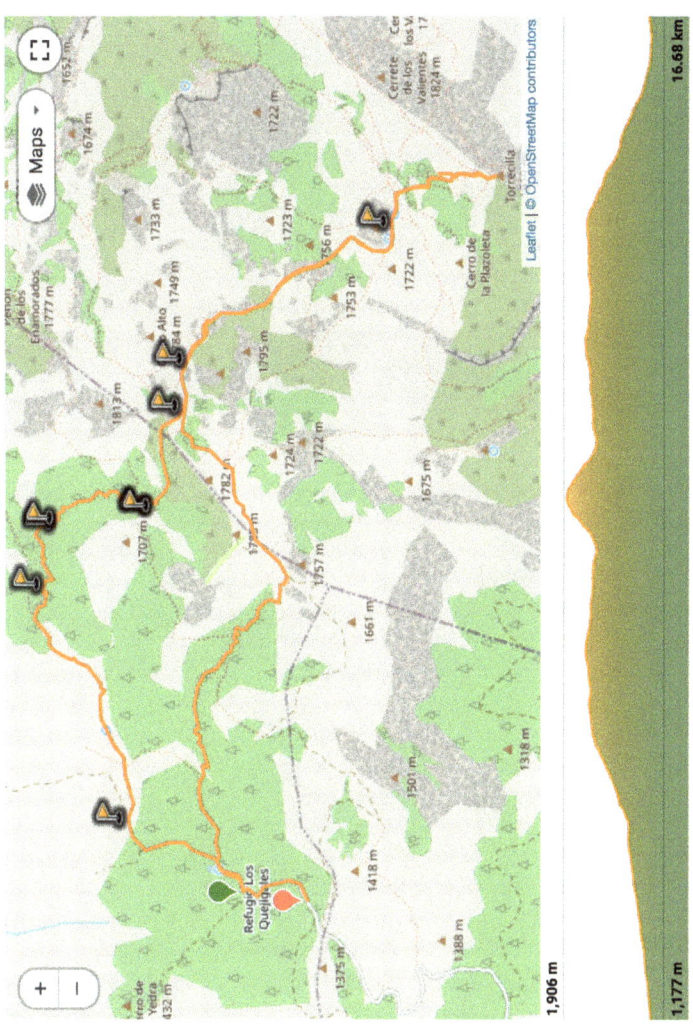

WALK 23: DOWN RONDA'S SPECTACULAR GORGE: A TASTE OF HISTORY AND WINE

Ronda is just a 45-minute drive from Marbella. It is the jewel of Andalucía and is one of the most-visited destinations in southern Spain. This well-preserved historic town is truly unique: it lies in a dramatic position on the edge of a 100-metre gorge called 'El Tajo'. The picturesque 'Puento Nuevo' bridge spans the Guadalevin river, which created a spectacular canyon that divides the city into the old Moorish quarter and the post-Reconquista modern town. The Moorish part has charming cobbled narrow streets with historic monuments such as the Arab baths and the medieval churches that were added at a later date. In the modern upmarket part of town, the streets are wider and have plazas. There's plenty of open space around the bullring in the Alameda del Tajo park, where you'll find the renowned balcony viewpoint hanging over the cliff.

Throughout history, the landscape of Ronda has provided security in turbulent times and was vital to the first tribes who settled here. The Celts were likely the first ones, but later the Romans and Moors turned it into a strong-walled fortified town. Given its defensive capabilities, it's no surprise that it was also one of the last towns to be taken from the Moors by the Spanish forces in 1485.

The Facts

Type:	Circular
Length:	8 kilometres
Level:	Easy
Elevation gain:	298 metres
Time:	2 hours

What to expect

A visit to Ronda is simply jaw-dropping, and this walk encompasses all the best views from above and below the gorge. There are roughly three parts to this walk. The first is a touristic stroll from the traditional bullring in the modern town, then along the breathtaking promenade over the bridges to the old town. You can sense the depth of the gorge from the various terraces and bridges. The far-reaching views to the rugged scenery around Ronda will thrill you in a way you'll never forget. As this part is also something of a stroll through history, you may want to budget for much more time than suggested so you can discover the many corners and points of interest. The second part gently descends the gorge on a wide well-paved footpath and then continues on a road in the valley. This part has exceptional views to the gorge and the Puente Nuevo bridge. The walk continues on a flatter country road between rural houses at the bottom of the gorge. It then goes back uphill on an easy forest path by the cliff and along the valley, where the unique Bodega Descalzos Viejos is located. The third part, if you wish, is the well-deserved and relaxing wine-tasting or 'cata de vino' in the bodega to finish off the walk and reflect on all you have learned and seen. Don't worry, you've almost finished your walk! But wine lovers should remember to book beforehand (http://www.descalzosviejos.com). The owner will happily guide you around and passionately tell you how he restored the beautiful chapel which houses the winery.

This walk is a wonderful introduction to further explorations in the stunning region of Ronda and the Serrania mountain range. Hopefully, it will give you a memorable first taste of the regions' wonderful culture, history, and nature.

History, stories and more...

The three original bridges and the famous New Bridge

Over the course of history, three bridges were built over the gorge in Ronda. The first one is the Moorish bridge, which is believed to have been built on Roman foundations. The second one, the Puente Viejo, was constructed in 1616 to connect the different parts of town. The Moors also built stairs down into the gorge to get water from the river. Only centuries later would the wider gap of the Tagus gorge be spanned. A first attempt was made under King Philip V of Spain, but the bridge collapsed causing the death of around 50 people. It took almost another 40 years (1793) to successfully complete today's masterpiece bridge, the 'Puento Nuevo' (New Bridge).

The emblematic bullring and bullfighting dynasties of Ronda

It was also under Philip V that bullfighting gained recognition under the nobles, and an enclosed space was needed. This gave birth to the elegant neo-classical bullring of Ronda in 1785, which is considered to be the birthplace of modern bull fighting. The Ronda school of bullfighting became one of the most renowned in the country because the toreros (bullfighters) fought on foot rather than on horseback, as was the tradition in Sevilla and Jerez. However, bullfighting is much older and can be traced back to as early as the 5th century AD, when it was a spectacle whereby young men taunted the animals to prove their strength and courage. Up to the 18th century, bullfighting took place wherever possible; on river banks, in squares, and in streets.

Ronda was also the birthplace of the first bullfighting dynasties represented by the Romero and Ordoñez families. Francisco Romero came up with the glorious idea of using a red cape to lead the bull. But Pedro Romero is seen as the most important figure in bullfighting history as he was the first to manage to elevate the position of a bullfighter in society outside the ring. He was immortalised by Francisco de Goya in his engravings. A copy of his work, the Tauromaquia, can be found in the bullring museum in Ronda. Bullfighting is deeply rooted in the Spanish culture, yet it has become very controversial in today's world, where this way of killing bulls is considered by many to be brutal.

An inspiration for artists

The beauty of Ronda has inspired writers and artists for centuries. Orson Welles and Ernest Hemingway were friends of Antonio Ordoñez and simply loved Ronda. Orson Welles was so fascinated that he requested his ashes to be brought here after his death. His memorial can be found at the Plaza de Toros.

Bodega region

Ronda has many bodegas and the tradition of winemaking in the region goes back to Roman times. Proof of this was found at the nearby archaeological site of Acinipo. The soil, altitude (750 metres), and climate provide wonderful conditions for viniculture. The bodegas produce young red wines, denominated Crianza and Tinto Joven, and are based on grape varieties such as Merlot, Sauvignon, Petit Verdot, Tempranillo, Syrah, Cabernet, and Romé. The most popular white wines, denominated Crianza and Blanca Joven, are created using Chardonnay, Macabeo, Colombard and Sauvignon Blanc grape varieties. If the wines meet certain requirements including location, preparation process, and the grape varieties used, they can apply to receive the Serrania de Ronda Denomination of Origin label. Enotourism attracts many people to the area every year. The Bodega Descalzos Viejos is conveniently located on the circular walk on the north side of Ronda. From the valley you can see across to the vineyards of this architectural pearl, which is built on the edge of the Tajo cliff. The current owners renovated the 16th-century Trinitarian convent, converted it into a bodega, and named it after the Order of the Barefoot Franciscans who once lived here.

Step-by-step guide

From the bullring, walk straight along the footpath next to the sculpture of Orson Welles to the viewpoint over the valley; then continue left on the cobbled Blas Infante promenade and by the parador until you reach the 'Puente Nuevo' bridge.

- Cross the Plaza de España into the narrow Calle Rosario.

- Go first right and down the Calle Virgen de los Remedios.

- Take the first right into Calle de la Mina. After a few metres, on the right, you'll find the entrance to the Jardines de Cuenca rose gardens, with amazing views along the gorge to the Puente Nuevo on one side and the countryside beyond the old bridge on the other side.

- Cross the small old Puente Viejo looking towards the gate built by Philip V.

- At the end of the bridge, turn immediately left onto the steps going down.

- Look straight ahead to the 13th-century Arab baths. They are the best preserved in Spain and follow the Roman model, with cold, warm, and hot-water rooms. Also look at the old Arab bridge on the left.

- Walk straight along the street from the Arab baths towards the walls.

- Turn right onto the footpath that goes up towards the walls.

- Stay on it, take a few steps up to the end of the footpath, and you'll see the 15th-century church called the Iglesia del Espiritu Santo.

- Follow the ramp up on the right and when you reach Calle Armiñan, go towards the right in the direction of the centre.

- After a few metres, turn left towards the Iglesia del Espiritu Santo in the Plaza Duquesa de Parcent. You'll enter this beautiful square with the town hall. The church itself was built on a mosque and took 200 years to finish.

- Cross the square into Manuel Montero alley and walk to the end.

- At Plaza Mondragon, turn left into Calle Ruedo Gamero.

- At Plaza Maria Auxiliadora, take the steps on the left and zigzag down into the valley with its spectacular view points of the gorge and town.

- At the wooden viewpoint, the walk continues on the left and follows the path through the little arch down into the valley. For a look closer at the gorge, follow the paths to the right before retracing your steps to continue the walk.

- Turn right on the cobbled road, which goes down gently, passing the albergue Los Molinos. At this point, you are also on a stretch of the Gran Senda de Malaga going towards the village of Benaoján.

- Keep left and head in the direction of Benaoján. The road goes up a little and then down to cross over the beautiful flowing water on the restored bridge, after which the road gradually ascends.

- Follow the tarmacked country road between rural houses and olive groves at the bottom of the impressive cliff, until you begin to climb up from the valley and head towards the plateau.

- Just after the turn, angle right onto a sandy path between pine trees and along the valley until you reach the last stretch back on the road leading to the town. The entrance to the Bodega Descalzos Viejos is on your right.

- Follow the road that bends back into town. You'll walk through a residential area with sport facilities on your left. You now walk on a paved footpath along the valley to take you back into town.
- At the Iglesia de la Merced, take a right into the Alamade de Tajo park to enjoy a refreshing stroll and some more viewpoints before ending the walk.

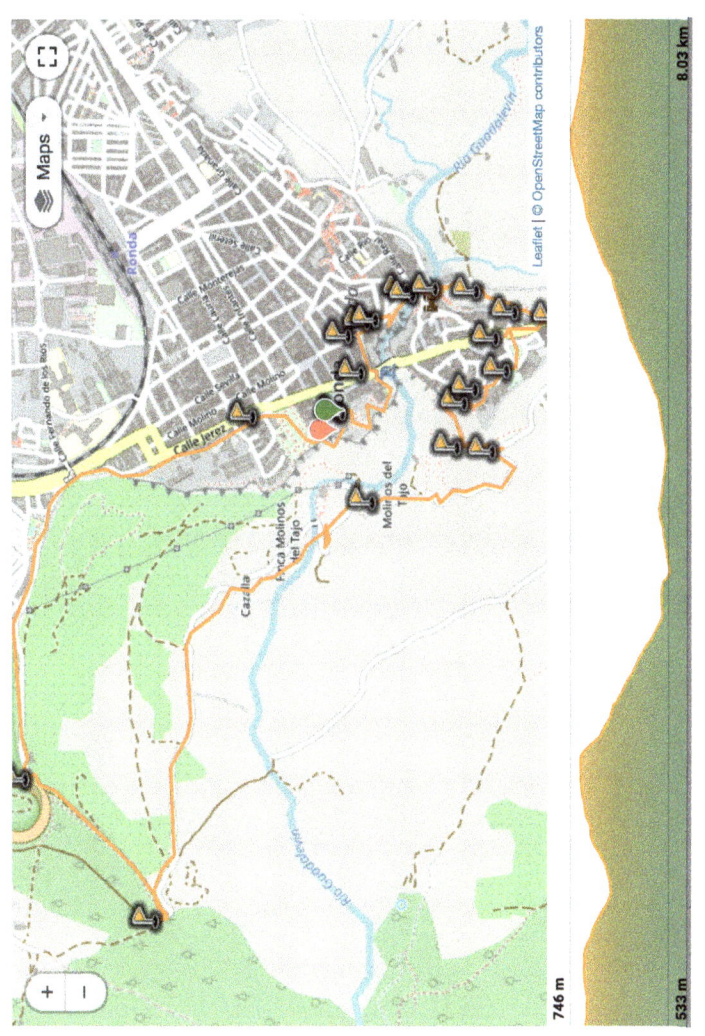

Walk 24: From Roman Acinipo to the Cave Houses of Setenil de las Bodegas

In the beautiful remote hills behind Ronda lies its best kept secret: the spectacular landmark ruins of the Roman amphitheatre of Acinipo. Only a short distance away are the magical cave houses of Setenil de las Bodegas surrounded by olive groves. This town is one of the most picturesque and unique in Cádiz province.

The Facts

Type:	Linear-one way
Length:	13 kilometres
Level:	Easy
Elevation gain:	110 metres
Time:	3.5 hours

What to expect

It's easy to fall in love with the landscape behind Ronda and the hill top on which Acinipo sits. There are splendid panoramic views over the mountain ranges of the three provinces that meet here: Málaga, Cádiz, and Sevilla. As far as the eye can see, there's just pure nature with only a few isolated houses here and there. The dramatic mountain tops of Grazalema are on one side and endless hills with olive groves on the other. Add a few stories and historical sites to this beautiful mix, and you have an absolutely unique walking experience running from the Roman Acinipo to Setenil de las Bodegas via the Ruta de los Bandoleros (the Bandit's Route). Make sure to take a full day out to fully explore the points of interest at the start and end of this walk.

The walk starts at the ruins of the Roman site of Acinipo. Note that the site is only open for visits in the morning (9 a.m. – 2.30 p.m., Wednesday to Sunday). After visiting the site, and with your mind full of Roman imagery, you start walking through the olive-covered hills. After passing a few isolated farm houses, you approach the river, where the scenery changes into lush forest and streams, which you'll have to cross a few times. This stretch must have been the ideal hideout for the 'bandoleros'. The last part goes up again through large olive groves and then goes down into the village. The path is easy and comfortable as it mainly runs flat through the countryside, but it offers little shade. Finish off with a well-deserved rest and local tapa dish at one of the terraces under the dramatic sun-lit caves at the 'Cuevas del Sol'. The restaurant staff will be happy to call a taxi for you if you haven't left a car at this point. The drive back from Setenil to Acinipo is very pleasant as the road is filled with bodegas attempting to attract the tourists. Some don't require booking, but others do. So if you have a specific bodega in mind, or just have to visit one, you must inquire in advance.

History, stories and more

Acinipo

Since prehistoric times, the presence of copper, iron, and lead has been exploited in the area. The Romans again knew why and where to settle when they constructed the fortified city of Acinipo over 2000 years ago (206 BC). Set in the middle of fertile land, Acinipo was strategically built at 999 metres to allow easy control of the surroundings and upper basins of the Guadiaro and Guadalete rivers. Acinipo became an important Roman city and even minted its own coins. It is believed that Acinipo used to be the old settlement of Ronda, hence its nickname 'Ronda la Vieja' (old Ronda). However, both Acinipo and Arunda (Ronda) existed at the same time. Still, Acinipo gradually lost importance to Arunda and around the 7th century it became deserted. The beautiful Roman amphitheatre had seating for about 2000 spectators. The builders took advantage of the slope and used local limestone rock to build the seating area and the area around it. Other visible remains include a 'domus' or stately home, with a special area for gymnastics, and some baths that used the natural springs at the site. Acinipo is a unique site and it is believed that what remains is only a fraction of what there is to be discovered and excavated.

Bandoleros

Banditry was known in the region of Andalucía especially in the 18th and 19th century, although it had always existed as a reaction against the established order. The bandoleros (bandits) were punished without mercy by being shot, hanged, or garrotted. Some of the stories about bandits described their violence, but others romanticised them as idealised figures fighting injustice, helping the poor by stealing from others, or battling social and political oppression as they did during the French invasion. They used the mountains of the Serrania de Ronda as a centre of operations. Some bandits became famous personalities, such as Juan José Mingolla, also known as 'Pasos Largos'. He was the last Andalucían bandolero, dying in 1934. If you want to find out more, the only museum fully dedicated to these bandoleros is in Ronda (www.museobandolero.org).

The cave houses of Setenil de las Bodegas

Setenil de las Bodegas is best known for the white town houses on the Calle de las Cuevas that were built into the huge canyon walls carved out by the river Trejo. The rocks form a natural pergola protecting the houses from extreme weather while keeping them fresh. Today, the houses of the Cuevas del Sol have been converted into bars and restaurants, which is a draw for tourists. It could be worthwhile to walk a bit further than the terraces because of possible renovation work going on. If so, you might be able to peek inside and see how incredibly small the interiors are. Setenil also has other wonderful monuments to visit, such as the Incarnación church and the 12th-century castle. It has just one tower left standing out of four and excellent views from the top.

Driving directions

To Acinipo

Acinipo is about 18 kilometres from Ronda. Leave Ronda, take the A-374 and then the MA-7402 to Setenil.

To Setenil

At the roundabout, just before Ronda and the bridge, drive straight towards Sevilla. Immediately after the roundabout, take the second exit onto the A-367. After a few hundred metres, take the turn onto the A-428 towards Setenil, which is signposted on the left. On the way to Setenil, you have to drive through a local village. The village with church in the distance is Setenil.

Step-by-step walking guide

- After visiting Acinipo, walk back down the road with its endless views over the hills covered with olive trees. Take the first left and continue until you reach a farm house and a ruined church.

- Go right here. This lane has a wooden sign 'Escuela de Campo'.

- Pass the rectangular fountain and stay on this country lane.

- At the turn, keep right (don't take the lane going up on the left). The lane curves along through the olive farms.

- At the next turn, angle left following the Setenil signpost.

- Cross the bridge over the river with the small waterfall.

- At the next turn, go left. At an old farmhouse, the path goes down on the left into a forest and you'll need to cross the river 'Rio de la Peña' twice. At the first crossing, you might have to take off your shoes.

- At the turn with the information board, keep straight on, and keep going straight on at the next one. The path widens and turns into a gravel road between large olive groves. At first, it goes up, but closer to the village it goes down.

- At the entrance of the village, take a left turn behind the bridge.

- Then go left along the river bank until you reach the bridge. From here, looking right, you can see the Cuevas del Sol with their inviting terraces. If you want to explore the village church and tower, continue along the Cuevas del Sol. But if you want to see the Cuevas de la Sombra (Caves of Shade), cross the small bridge at the cave houses.

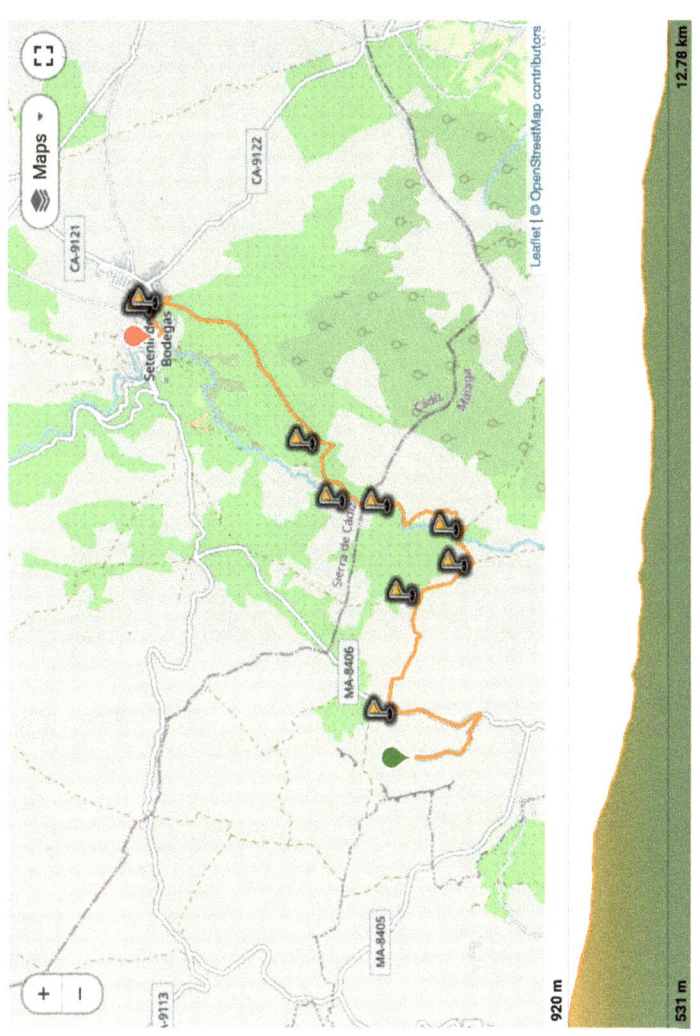

WALK 25: CAT'S CAVE MOUNTAIN CIRCUIT NEAR BENAOJÁN (SIERRA GRAZALEMA)

In the middle of super-dry southern Spain, there's a region that surprisingly accounts for more rainfall than the rest of the peninsula: the Sierra de Grazalema. This beautiful mountain range is a natural park of 53,411 ha covering 14 municipalities north-east of Cádiz and north-west of Málaga. It has many wonderful hiking paths. The most challenging is the hike to the peak of El Torreón (1,654 m), which is the highest in Cádiz. The karstic limestone mountains are rugged and grey and are threaded with dozens of rivers and caverns. They are an underground paradise for caving and canyoning, especially the more well-known Cueva de Pileta, Cueva del Gato (Cat's Cave), and la Garganta Verde. The caves are also a favourite habitat of no less than 19 different types of bats.

The white village of Benaoján lies at 564 metres on the eastern border of Grazalema between the beautiful green Guadiaro valley and the Sierra de Benaoján (Málaga Province). It covers 32 square kilometres and has a population of around 1,700.

The Facts

Type:	Circular
Length:	7.89 kilometres
Level:	Moderate
Elevation gain:	241 metres
Time:	2.5 hours

What to expect

With its emerald-green lagoon, the Cueva del Gato is one of the most beautiful sites in the immense Sierra de Grazalema Natural Park. It lies at the foot of a mountain range within walking distance of Benaoján. It is also quite close to Montejaque and within easy reach of Ronda. You can park the car in front of the cave if that's all you wish to do. Here we take a circular walk that includes the cave and then heads up the mountain. The walk can be roughly divided into three different parts. The first part starts at the legendary Bobadilla-Algeciras rail station in Benaoján and follows an easy flat path along the banks of the Guadiaro river before it reaches the cave. The next part is a steeper climb up the hill of Los Pajarejos followed by a gentler climb on an old cobblestone path by a cliff wall with a very deep drop. This means that this walk is unsuitable for children or beginner hikers. The third part goes back down to the Benaoján, with stunning views of the village and Montejaque, before it reaches the village centre and the Camino del Rio (river walk), which takes you back to the railway station. This linear village is built along the side of a steep mountain slope and has a tiny centre with a 15th-century parish church.

History, stories and more

Cueva del Gato

The Cat's Cave is the southern mouth of the largest Andalucían caving labyrinth called the Hundidero-Gato system with its permanent water and lagoons. Thanks to the cave painting of a yellow deer and an archaeological site inside the cave, we can retrace the presence of humans to at least Palaeolithic times some 18,000 years ago. Today, the lagoon or 'Charco Frío' in front of the cave is an ideal place to cool off during the hot summer months. The ice-cold water comes from the Gaduares River that has travelled through kilometres of underground caves before flowing into the Guadiaro River. The Cueva del Gato was declared an Andalucían natural monument in 2011.

Roman path

There's a 200-metre stretch on the walk that represents the remains of a Medieval path which was built on a previous Roman path. The Roman way connected the cities of Carteia in San Roque and Acinipo in Ronda via the valley of Guadiaro.

Victorian railway

The Benaoján railway station has obvious English colonial features which reveal its surprising origin. Mr Henderson, an

Englishman, financed the challenging project of connecting the 178 kilometres between Algeciras and Bobadilla. The line was successfully inaugurated in 1892 after astonishing engineering work over rivers and cutting through mountain ranges. In those days and places, banditry was still very active. But it was worthwhile because it opened up a huge trade opportunity for products coming from North Africa into Algeciras, then from Bobadilla to Madrid, and then to the rest of the world (not forgetting Britain).

Driving directions

It takes about 1 hour 20 minutes to drive from Marbella to Benaoján. Take the Ronda road from San Pedro de Alcántara until reaching the roundabout before the centre of Ronda. Then take the A-374 to Sevilla, followed by the MA-7401 to Benaójan. The drive from Ronda is very scenic (16 kilometres) and the destination very well worth the effort.

Step-by-step walking guide

- The walk starts at the Benaoján railway station, which is about 1.5 kilometres outside the village and clearly signposted.

- In front of the station, walk right for about 100 metres and turn left to cross the railway.

- Take the first street on the left at the building with the phrase 'Los Cachones' written on it. Go along the street to the end and continue on the narrow forest path next to the river.

- Cross the Guadiaro river on the stepping stones.

- After crossing, take a left turn onto a country road by the river.

- You'll get to a rural hostel, originally an ancient mill, where the path continues straight along by the wall of the hostel. The path narrows and briefly climbs. Here are the remains of the original Roman and later medieval path.

- Where the path bends there is a pond called Charco Redondo. Nearer to the Cueva del Gato hotel there's a wooden bridge which you cross over the Guadiaro River. It was broken the last time we went, but it's easy to cross the river and follow the wooden footpath under the tunnel.

- A few metres further on is the stunning green lagoon of Cueva del Gato.

- In the open space in front of the lagoon, there's a narrow path that goes up. It goes up gently. If you find yourself climbing steeply, you may have walked off the path. It gradually curves up and then takes a sharp left turn where it joins the rocky path along the cliff wall. Halfway along you can already see the hill you are heading to.

- The path on the cliff is easy and wide enough, but there is no railing on the left and the deep fall is dangerous. However, it's only a small stretch and you'll soon reach a farmhouse gate.

- At the farmhouse, the cliff path ends and takes a sharp turn inland, where it continues on a country road between farmland. It then starts to zigzag sharply going down. This is where you can see the fabulous landscape of the limestone cliffs with Montejaque on your right and Benaoján in front.

- Continue straight on until you reach a turn.

- Turn left at the bridge over the Arroyo Montejaque. Walk through small farmhouses and the industrial area of the village.

- Closer to the village, keep left on the long descending road.

- Again, go left downhill on the road alongside small town houses (alternatively, you can go straight through the village centre). The trail leaves the centre and crosses the river again.

- After a short stretch on the road, walk on the footpath on the right and take the first exit on a dirt road going down to the river.
- Take the first street on the left, where you enter a small picturesque area with hostels.
- After a few metres, take the first left.
- Cross the river and take a right turn to end at the railway and the station on your left.

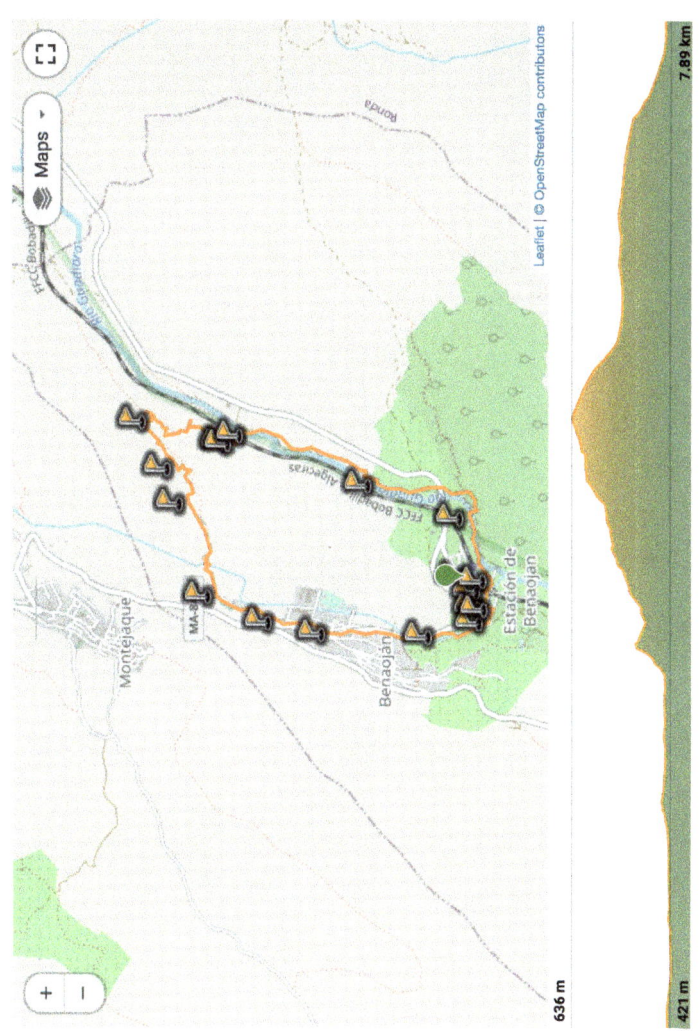

Chestnut Paradise: The Valle del Genal, South of Ronda

With the arrival of autumn, walking the colourful chestnut-covered hills of the Valle del Genal is a must. This region south of Ronda includes about 3,800 hectares of chestnut trees that colour the landscape in coppery tones of ochre, brown, yellow, and orange. The area extends over the white villages of the Valle del Genal (Genal Valley) in the Serrania de Ronda. In October, people work very hard in the otherwise rather silent villages and everyone is involved. Almost all the locals have chestnut groves that have been passed on over generations, ranging from smaller plots to larger domains of 30 hectares or more. The working day starts early and in the afternoon the harvest is sold on the basis of weight, size, and quality. Lorries drive up and down all day. The best chestnuts for sale are neatly packed in local factories and exported all around the world.

Spain is the 9th-largest producer and exporter of chestnuts worldwide. Not bad when you know that the villages are very small. They produce about 4 million kilos per year of a specific chestnut, called 'pilonga' which means 'easy to peel'. The Genal Valley is Málaga's largest producer and is responsible for 70% of Andalucía's total harvest. Within the valley, the largest producers are in Pujerra, Igualeja, and Parauta, although other nearby villages, such as Genalguacil, Jubrique, Algatocin, and Cartajima, also contribute significant amounts. Three villages in the nearby Sierra de las Nieves—Yunquera, Ojén and Istán—also count with chestnut trees. After all, the mountainous landscape and climate are ideal for growing this type of tree. The quality of this tasty nut is highly regarded in countries such as Italy, France, the United Kingdom, and Germany.

How did it all start? Once again, with the Romans, who first harvested these trees. But it's only since the 1950s that this industry has grown into the one we know today. So, these trees have a well-established history, which explains why you can find really beautiful old ones between 300 and 500 years old. The most famous is the Castaño Santo (Holy Chestnut) in Istán, which is estimated to be between 800 and 1000 years old.

After all the hard work, the farmers celebrate, after all we are in Spain! And everyone is welcome. The picking season ends around November 1st and many villages celebrate the traditional Tostón festival, when they roast chestnuts and make all kinds of dishes based on these tasty nuts. At this time, the doors of the tiny chestnut museum in Pujerra will be open. To add some extra flavour, they offer wines from the region!

Where to walk

There are many hikes to choose from in the Genal Valley and we only present a fraction of them. For families with smaller children, the Cartajima-Júzcar walk is a winner. A more intense one is the Parauta-Igualeja trail, a roller-coaster walk up and down the hills. If that isn't challenging enough, expert hikers are welcome to use their creativity and connect three villages or more to quickly make a challenging 5-hour hike. To make access easy, we describe the starting points at Parauta and Cartajima because they are close to the Ronda road. As a treat, you can buy packs of chestnuts at the factory on Avenida Rey Fernando VII in Cartajima.

Driving directions

Take the A-397 from San Pedro de Alcántara and head in the direction of Ronda. Drive for about 35 minutes, pass the Igualeja turn and fuel station, and take a left turn at the Parauta and Cartajima exit on the MA-7306, 11 kilometres south of Ronda. The narrow access road cuts through the Serrania de Ronda mountains and makes the drive fun and a true pleasure for the eyes. You can easily park your car on the outskirts of the villages.

Walk 26: From Cartajima to the Smurf village of Júzcar

The Facts

Type:	Linear
Length:	8.58 kilometres return
Level:	Easy/moderate
Elevation gain:	397 metres
Time:	2 hours return

What to expect

The Cartajima–Júzcar route is ideal for walkers of all levels including children. This trail will definitely motivate the little ones in autumn because chestnuts cover the roads and can be easily collected. As a bonus, they can see the blue-painted village of Júzcar with lots of fun features including a zip line over the village. In contrast to Cartajima, which is rather quiet, Júzcar has lots of terraces where you can have a snack or lunch. The white village of Cartajima, at 846 metres, has a superb location at the foot of a spectacular limestone karst landscape called 'Los Riscos' in the Sierra de Oreganal above the Alto Genal valley. While walking through chestnut groves, the views to the rugged cliffs will accompany you on the majority of the walk until you reach Júzcar and its striking blue colour.

The hike is easy but rated moderate because it has steep parts both up and down which demand extra effort, especially on your return. A stroll in the steep streets of Júzcar will add to this challenge. The people of Cartajima are very friendly and you might be allowed to peek into the factory (which is on your way), where the chestnuts are mechanically selected and packed by machines making a loud drumming sound. Picking some chestnuts here and there during your walk doesn't hurt, but it's nice to support the local industry by buying a few bags.

Cannonballs and tinplate

Inscriptions on the facades of houses in Cartajima unravel some of the curious history and culture of this village. Its origins go back to the Romans and Phoenicians, although it mainly bears traces of the Moorish period. The name Cartajima suggests that the village was most likely the holding of a large family as it means 'Homestead of Aljaima.' It remained a Muslim village until just after the Christian conquest in 1492, when it became a parish with a church. In the 19th century, Cartajima flourished by exploiting the iron deposits and manufacturing cannonballs. It was called 'Little Cadiz'. Today, only about 200 people live there.

History, stories and more

The Smurf village: Juzcár

For a long time, chestnuts have been the main source of income for the whole region, until something extraordinary happened to the hidden-away white village of Júzcar. In 2011, all the houses in the village were painted light blue! Why blue? Sony Pictures had decided to celebrate the premiere of their Smurf movie in Júzcar and so 4,000 litres of Smurfy-blue paint converted the village into the magic Smurf town called 'El Pueblo de los Pitufos'. Overnight, the village became an attraction for thousands of visitors, instead of the usual couple of hundred per year. After the promotional period, the 200 locals, who welcomed the blue gold the Smurfs had brought them, voted to keep the houses blue. Since then, more than 50,000 tourists per year are economically boosting not only Júzcar but also the rest of the region, which mainly lives on the chestnut industry. However, as happens in many fairy tales, their luck turned. Since the 15th of August 2017, they lost their status as the Smurf village. International Merchandising Promotion & Services (IMPS) invoked their right to the commercial use of the Smurf brand, which was based on the comic series created in 1958 by the Belgian cartoonist Pierre Culliford, nicknamed 'Peyo'. So, Júzcar had to remove Smurf-related statues and anything connected with the use of the brand. However, the houses can stay blue for as long as the locals wish. Luckily, Sony Pictures negotiated with the IMPS for Júzcar to be able to keep some of the images painted on the facades of buildings. It remains to be seen if Júzcar and the region will continue to build on their previous success as the Smurf village.

Its Smurf glory aside, the 18th century was probably the most significant for Júzcar as it experienced an economic boom due to the construction of a tinplate factory, which was the first of its kind in Spain.

Step-by-step walking guide

- Walk from the Los Castaños hotel at the entrance to Cartajima to the centre on the Avenida Rey Fernando VII. You pass sports facilities and the chestnut factory on the right-hand side of the road.

- Take the second street on the right (don't go left down the hill) leading to the beautiful 16th-century church of Nuestra Señora del Rosario.

- Opposite the church stairs, walk down the street on the right.

- Immediately turn right again into Calle Padre Francisco Rodriguez Gallego (the name is longer than the street!), which ends with views to the valley.

- Turn right onto Calle Nueva and keep left while walking downhill out of the village with its views of the valley.

- Before continuing, you can take a 300-metre detour to the right to see the Fuente de los Peces (Fish Fountain), which was originally constructed by Moors. Locals used to collect their water here before running water reached the houses.

- If you skipped the detour, go straight on and go right (twice), where you'll find yourself going downhill on a country road between chestnut trees. You can see the stunning rocks of Los Riscos over on your right. You reach the lowest point of the trail at the Cañada del Arroyo Blanco.

- After crossing this dry river, the path climbs between holm oaks. Initially, the path narrow and rocky, but then widens again to become a dirt road until it reaches a tarmacked road.

- On this road (the MA-7303), turn left and walk for about 100 metres until there is an open space on the right.

- Leave the road on your right-hand side, then turn immediately left and go down into the village, while enjoying your first glimpse of some blue-painted houses.

- Of course, how long you stay and explore the village is entirely up to you. Just allow yourself 1 hour to return the same way you came.

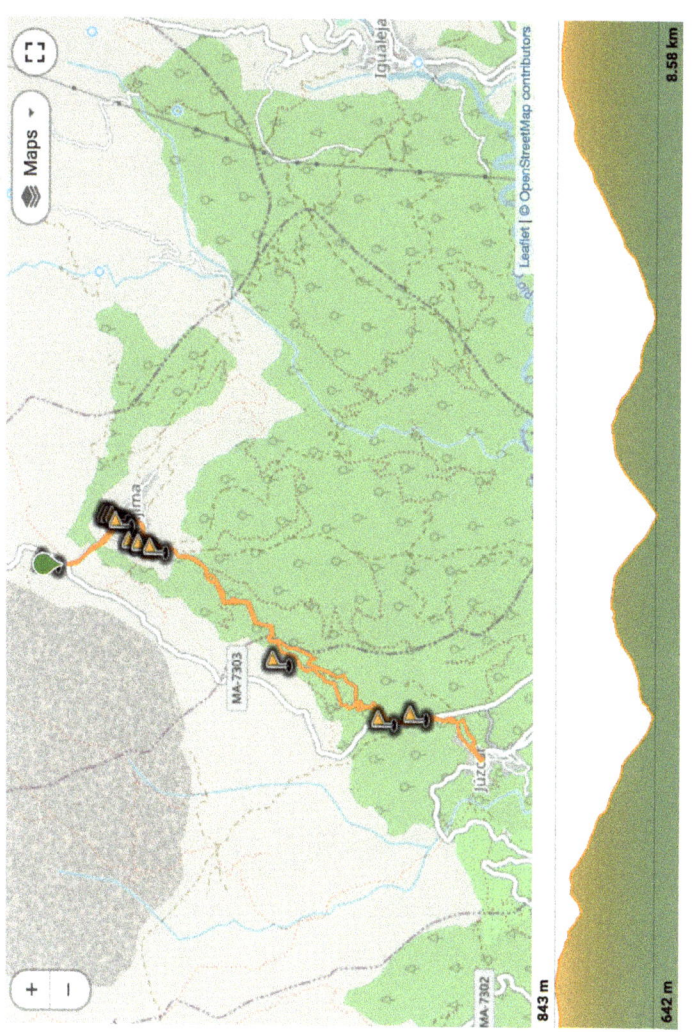

Walk 27: Chestnut route: Igualeja-Parauta

The Facts

Type:	Circular
Length:	13.24 kilometres
Level:	Moderate
Elevation gain:	592 metres
Time:	3.5 hours

What to expect

This varied intense walk takes you through the chestnut-covered hills of two white villages in the Genal Alto valley. Although the altitude difference between Parauta at 799 m and Igualeja at 706 m may not seem much, the elevation gain on this walk is quite high (592 m) because the walk follows the ups and downs of the steep hills around the villages. There are roughly two parts to this walk. From Parauta, it begins with a deep descent on a winding country road between chestnut groves until reaching a river, which you cross. Part of the trail then climbs on a mix of dirt roads and forest trails. About halfway on the walk, you reach the larger village of Igualeja, the second-largest chestnut producer. You can have a break here at the source of the Rio Genal or the Rio Nacimiento (River of Birth). The second part is the return hike. The path is less well indicated and mainly runs on dirt roads until it reaches the river, which you cross twice, in the valley between Cartajima and Parauta. The last stretch is a final climb up the steep hill towards Parauta. A very welcome Mirador (Viewpoint) awaits you on your arrival in Parauta, where you have the most amazing views of Cartajima, which is surrounded by a carpet of copper in autumn, with Los Riscos in the distance.

History, stories and more

Parauta's tiny monuments

The tiny ancient Arab arch on the village square used to be the entrance to the village during the Moorish period. The Iglesia de la Purisima Concepción church dates back to the 16th century and has some fascinating aspects such as the Mudéjar-style tower and an 18th-century statue of the Virgin Mary. According to legend, Santa María (St. Mary) saved a fish seller and his donkey from drowning when he was filling his baskets with fish to sell in the villages of the valley. When he later visited Parauta, he saw the church gate open and upon entering the church found the statue of María with the same facial features as his rescuer and with sand at her feet.

Genal river

The Genal river is important to the region as it supplies water to fifteen municipalities and their marvellous landscapes. Its source is in a cave known as El Nacimiento (The Birth) in Igualeja. It was declared a Natural Monument for its environmental value. The source of the Rio Genal is at the entrance to the village.

Step-by-step guide

- Park at the Mirador de la Era and walk along Calle del Calvario to the centre.

- Take the first street on the left going up the hill away from the centre.

- Keep left at the next turn. From here the road starts to strongly climb between chestnut groves. You can also see some impressive cork oaks.

- Cross the Arroyo de los Granados stream, which is very easy. You are now at the lowest point of the walk at 675 m.

- After a few metres, you reach an open area where you have to take a right turn and go along a grass-covered path.

- The path takes you over a wooden bridge, after which there is a dirt road with large holes.

- At the next turn, keep walking straight and go down into the valley. There is a signpost on the right that could confuse you because it says Ruta Castaños (Chestnut Route). However, this is a short circuit next to Igualeja, which we partly walk on when returning.
- When you enter the village, turn right twice and then left at the shop. Follow Calle del Canal which winds down through the centre.
- Take a left at the car park and follow the river, cross the bridge, and then turn left at the main square with the Igualeja fountain. At the end of this street is the small park, cave, and source of the Rio Genal.
- Trace your steps back to the Igualeja fountain and continue straight on, passing the 16th-century Santa Rosa de Lima church.
- Turn right into Calle Ermita, where there is a small chapel. Take the road on the right of the chapel to reach the car park again.
- Take the first street on left (Calle Hiladero) and walk out of the village again.
- Turn right twice and follow the signpost 'Ruta Castaños'. This is a narrow footpath with large holes, so please take care. It ends in a wider dirt road.
- Turn right onto a tarmacked rural lane.
- Further up keep on the left.
- Then keep right on the dirt road.
- Continue straight on at the next turn.
- Keep left at the next fork.
- Turn right at the next fork. The path strongly climbs again towards the river. There are some steeper parts in the forest.
- Cross the river, which is easy. Then walk right towards

the tall trees. The road bends and you have to cross the river again.

- Now it is just a question of zigzagging up a country road to Parauta, passing a flatter grassy area.

- As you enter the village at the Mirador, take the street on the right (Calle Salvador Marqués). At the village square, turn into the second street on the left. Keep on this street until it takes you out of the village again you reach the car park.

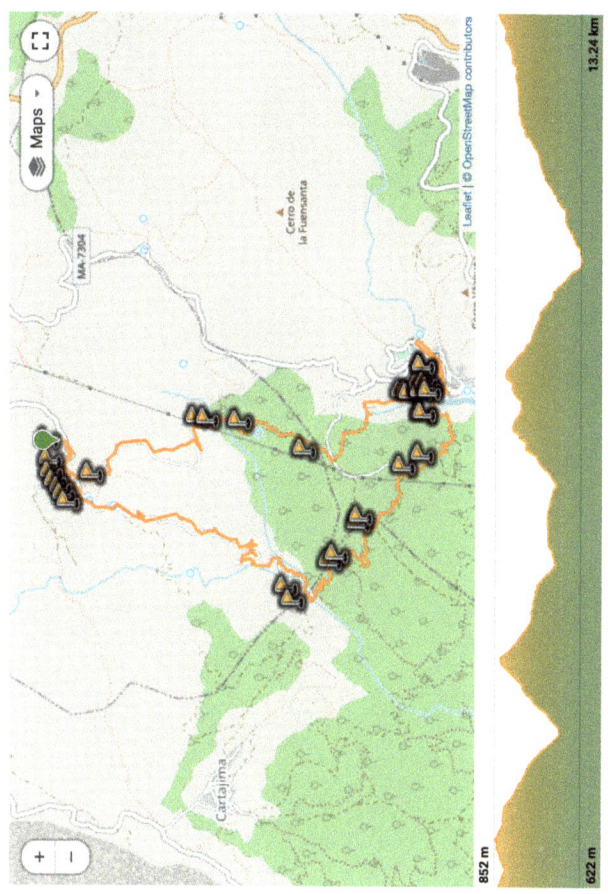

3.2. DIRECTION ESTEPONA & INLAND

WALK 28: AWARD-WINNING ART AND HILLS OF THE GENALGUACIL 'MUSEO PUEBLO'

Creativity comes in many ways and it's very impressive how Genalguacil came up with the idea of becoming an open-air art museum to draw tourists to their tiny remote village on the western side of the Genal valley. The village is very deeply nestled in the valley within the foothills of the Sierra Bermeja and just 40 kilometres from Ronda. After a scenic drive through the mountains and other villages of the Serrania de Ronda, it takes a focused driver to navigate the last stretch as the roads curve sharply down into the valley. Genalguacil is worth the effort because of all the original contemporary art works placed around this village set within mountainous surroundings. This initiative has rightly made Genalguacil famous and it's known as the Museo Pueblo (Village Museum). At the time of writing, in May 2021, the village was included in the list of the 'Most Beautiful Towns in Spain' at the Fitur international tourism fair in Madrid.

The Facts

Type:	Circular
Length:	5.72 kilometres
Level:	Easy
Elevation gain:	314 meters
Time:	1.5 hours

What to expect

Even if you are not extremely passionate about art, you might change your mind when exploring Genalguacil, where art is integrated into the village in a fun, creative, and aesthetic way. Allow plenty of time to discover the art works hiding around each corner. Combine your explorations with a touch of nature and

splendid views by taking this short walk outside the village. The natural surroundings will delight you, and if you visit in autumn you'll be amazed by the gorgeous colours, because Genalguacil is in the heart of the chestnut region. The art adventure starts immediately when you arrive because you have to walk through the village to find the start of the path into the hills. Having inspired your mind, you can then completely disconnect by walking the circuit around the village through chestnuts, olives, and cork trees. The walk is easy, mainly runs over wide dirt roads, and only has gentle ups and downs. There are beautiful mountain views at all times, but that means you are also very exposed to the sun. When you get back at the entrance to the village, you may like to take a bit more time to discover yet more art works and pay a visit to the museum.

History, stories and more

Artist residency

Since 1994, Genalguacil has held the 'Encuentro de Arte' (Art Encounter) every 2 years. The quiet village is transformed into a busy art event with a full programme of artistic workshops for all audiences. This is also when the artists can bask in glory and proudly present the works they've made in and for the village. Different personalities from the art world carefully choose the art projects from among the many applications from national and international artists. Once the artists have been selected, they are invited to spend time in the remote mountain village with accommodation, living expenses, materials, and a small payment provided by the municipality. In this way, the artists can work peacefully and use the best of their creative energy to create art projects that blend in or stand out in the village streets. The materials used are also frequently sourced from the region.

National and international recognition

After the event, the art works remain on permanent public display in the streets. In this manner, Genalguacil has gradually built up a very valuable cultural heritage of no less than 160 different works of art. Around half of them are scattered around the streets and the other half are housed in the Museo de Arte Contemporáneo Fernando Centeno López (Contemporary Art Museum). This museum opened its doors in 2004 and is based in an old olive oil mill.

This is the way the Genalguacil Museum strongly competes with more well-known ones, such as the Picasso Museum in Málaga. For example, it was included in the list of Spain's top 100 cultural hotspots and was mentioned in the New York Times in 2014.

And more…

There's barely 500 Genalguacileños (have a go at pronouncing this!) and even then you hardly see any of them. It's no wonder that the village has a department fully dedicated to the depopulation problem, which is a typical issue in tiny rural villages. Genalguacil is certainly peaceful out of season! The pronunciation of the name of the village reveals its Arab origins, as it is derived from 'Genna-Alwacir', meaning the Gardens of the Vizier. The name also refers to the river Genal, which has always been of importance to the region's agricultural industry.

Driving directions

It's about a 1.5-hour drive from Marbella to Genalguacil. This may seem long but note that the journey is very scenic as it cuts through the mountains. There are two recommended ways to get there. The first and longer one is via Estepona over the Sierra Bermeja mountain. We describe the other route, which cuts through villages such as Casares, Algatocin, and Gaucin. Take the AP-7 motorway in the direction of Algeciras and take the exit to Gaucin. Once in Gaucin centre, the road ends at a crossing. Go left and then immediately right at the petrol station, heading in the direction of Ronda (A-369). At Algatocin, drive through this village and follow the road to Genalguacil (MA-8305). After 14 kilometres of roads winding down into the valley, you will be welcomed by the first art works.

Step-by-step guide

- The hike starts right at the entrance of the village, just behind the tiny car park.

- Find the start of the path by heading to Calle Lomilla behind the church. At the village entrance, follow Calle Real to the main square (Plaza de la Constitución), which you cross. Enjoy the fantastic views, then go down a smaller street on the left for a few metres. Then go left up the street until you reach Calle Lomilla.

- Walk along this street, which leads you out of the village. Behind the car park and art fountain, leave the road and walk uphill on a dirt road signposted to Los Saucillos.

- Cut sharp left and climb a forest path with an old wooden board saying 'Camino'. Follow this footpath, keeping on the right and passing some impressive cork oaks until it turns into a wider vehicle-accessible dirt road.

- At the next turn, take a left up the road, which gently climbs and keep left again. At this point, you'll find yourself among lots of chestnut trees.

- Further up the path, go left at the green and white signpost to make your way back to the village. The white dots you can see on the mountain slopes in the distance are the nearby villages.

- At the end of the path, take a sharp left and end back in the village at the starting point, angling right at the picturesque blue and white house and sculpture of a man sitting and looking through an empty picture frame, thus drawing attention to the amazing views of the natural landscape in front of him.

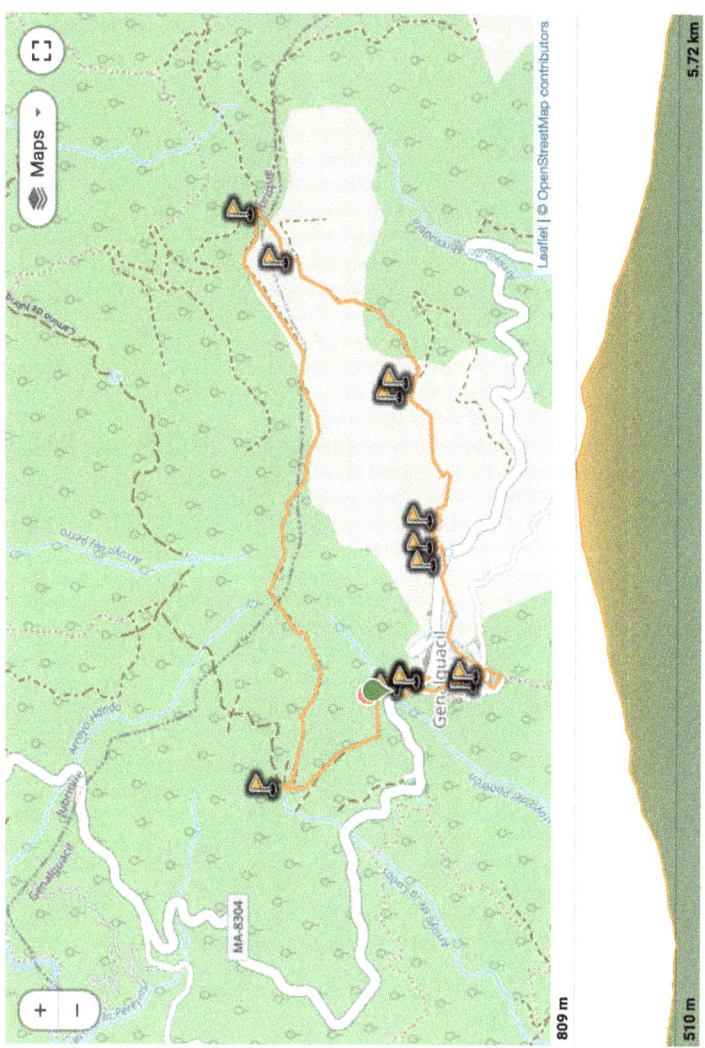

WALK 29: CANYON OF THE VULTURES : ALCORNOCALES PARK

The Cañon de Las Buitreras (Canyon of the Vultures) is one of the most scenic spots in the area. It lies at the edge of Los Alcornocales (The Cork Trees) Natural Park in the municipality of Cortes de la Frontera. The abundance of rain in this area and the large network of rivers and streams have created extraordinary landscapes with so-called 'canutos' or long deep ravines. On the eastern side lies the 4-kilometre Cañon de Las Buitreras, which was gradually carved out by the Rio Guadiaro million of years ago. The stunning vertical walls of the canyon can be over 200 metres deep and are the favourite nesting site of griffon vultures (also known as buitre leonado). These impressive scavengers gave the canyon its name. At some points the canyon is so narrow that the walls almost touch. The Cañon de Las Buitreras is one of the most spectacular canyons in Andalucía and has been declared a Natural Monument. The long watercourse makes it a great spot for canyoning. However, this more adventurous activity must be done with a professional guide and with authorisation.

The Facts

Type:	Linear
Length:	10 kilometres
Level:	Easy
Elevation gain:	378 metres
Time:	3 hours

What to expect

This beautiful linear walk runs on a path parallel to and above the Rio Guadiaro leading to the south side of the Cañon de Las Buitreras. You'll be able to see the impressive canyon from the emerald green waters as well as from above. The elevation gain is not too demanding as some parts of the path are flatter. Higher up, at the Mirador de las Buitreras (Griffon

Vultures' Viewpoint), you can spot the vultures flying above you or resting on the enormous cliff opposite the viewpoint. You'll be glad you brought your binoculars as you'll be able to see their nests. This point is really one of the best to get as close as possible to these intimidating but impressive creatures. Their dramatic circling above our heads made us feel happy we left the dog at home! After the mirador, the path climbs to the highest point with the big rocks, where the views down to the river are excellent. The path is easily accessible and there's a wooden hanging bridge to cross over. You'll also see a concrete railway tunnel on this route.

History, stories and more

Alcornocales oak tree park

The canyon is situated in the Alcornocales park, which has greatest number of cork trees and the best gall oak forests in the entire Iberian Peninsula. Despite this unique biodiversity, the park is not as well known and visited as other natural parks in Andalucía. However, the area is far from small, spanning more than 167,767 ha in the provinces of Málaga and Cádiz, and includes 17 municipalities which are all part of Cádiz Province except for Cortes de la Frontera. The highest peak (1,092 metres) is in the Sierra de Aljibe. To the north is the Sierra de Grazalema (close to Ronda) and to the south is the area around Gibraltar. The forest also includes trees such as the myrtle, kermes oak, wild olive, and palmetto. The palmetto is the only native European palm tree and can grow up to 2 metres.

Cork oaks have an outer layer that is spongy, waterproof, and elastic. This is ideal for making corks, which has been done since Roman and Greek times. Cork now has a variety of commercial uses, such as for flooring, insulation, decoration, and more. Every 9 to 12 years, the cork layers are carefully cut off by experts, called 'peladores' (peelers), in the early mornings of the hot summer months. Out walking, it's fairly common to encounter a farmer with his donkey loaded with a huge pile of these slices. If you want to see the cork trees you have to go deeper into the park or visit in the hills around the villages of the Genal valley.

Hydroelectric plant

Since 1919, the hydroelectric power station of Las Buitreras has been using the water of the Guadiaro to produce renewable electricity. At the time, it provided the first long-distance high-voltage cable that transmitted electricity to Sevilla. It would later grow into a network that distributed electricity to the entire country.

Griffon Vultures

You'll be captivated by this colossal bird of prey (Gyps Fulvus) with its wing-span reaching up to 2.5 metres and weighing in at around 10 kilos. Its colours range from a contrasting white to dark ochre, cinnamon, and brown with very tiny white feathers on the neck and head. Their curved beaks, a characteristic of all raptors, are used to tear meat into shreds. This bird is mainly found in mountainous areas and cliffs in southern Europe and in

parts of Asia and Africa. This day bird likes to stay in the same habitat and flies very high soaring over long distances searching for dead animals. They're also great team players, because when one bird spots food, the rest of the colony joins in.

Driving directions

The starting point of the walk is just over an hour's drive from Marbella. Take the AP-7 motorway towards Algeciras and then take the exit to Gaucin on the A-377. After reaching Gaucin, turn left, then left again at the petrol station onto the A-405. Drive for about 2 kilometres, then turn right onto the MA-512 until reaching El Colmenar. Park at the station.

Step-by-step walking guide

- At the entrance of El Colmenar, follow the street to the right with the signpost 'CH Buitreras'.

- Turn right and follow the road between beautiful trees aligned in rows until reaching the hydroelectric power station. The walk starts on the left.

- Walk a few metres up along the pipeline; a shockingly ugly start, but very short.

- Turn right under the pipeline and continue on the narrow sandy path, which gradually climbs and passes an old irrigation channel. It's very easy to follow. After about 40 minutes, take the short deviation to the lagoon in the canyon. Afterwards, retrace your steps and then continue on the same path.

- The walk stops at the Mirador. However, the path continues for about 500 metres downhill until it reaches the Puente de los Alemanes. This was built in 1918 to carry water to the electric power station. IMPORTANT! This point is very dangerous and should not be crossed.

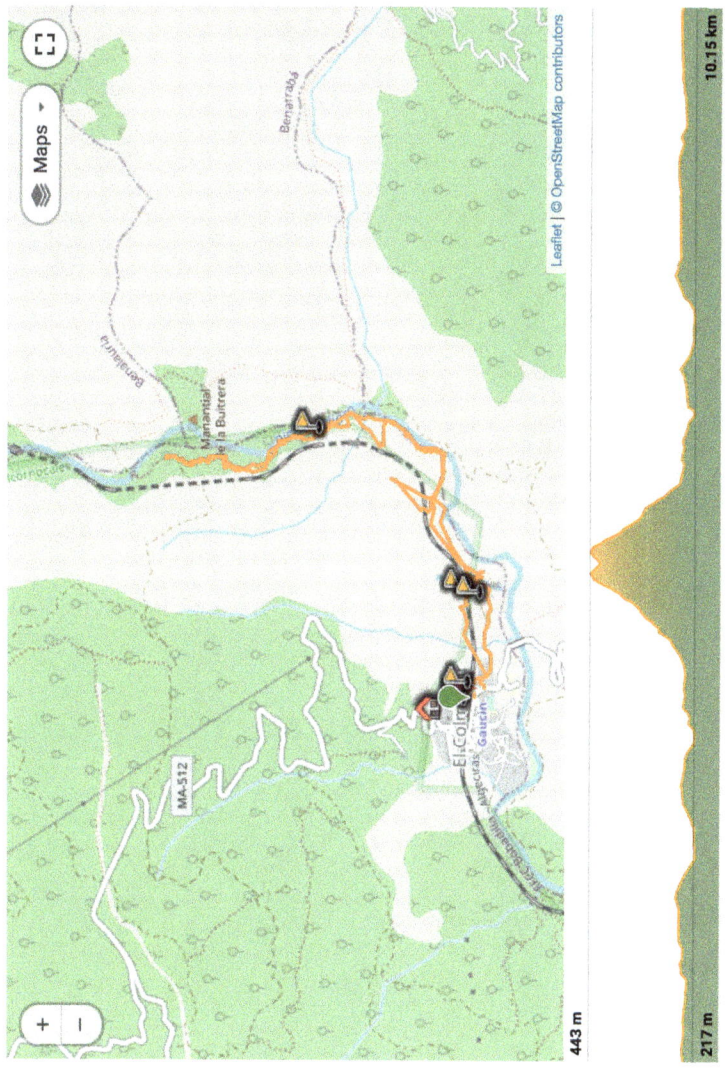

WALK 30: MAJESTIC CLIFF VILLAGE OF CASARES: CRESTELLINA MOUNTAIN VIEWS AND SUMMIT WALK

The little white houses of the village of Casares elegantly cling to a steep cliff crowned with the ruins of a 13th-century Arab castle. There are grass-green valleys and hills, dramatic cliffs, and sea views in the distance. The municipality stretches from the coast at Casares Costa and climbs up to the village, which is nestled at the foot of the Sierra Crestellina. It lies between several mountain ranges: the Sierra Bermeja behind Estepona, the Valle Genal towards Ronda, and the Sierra Alcornocales towards Cádiz. This natural setting alone makes the village stand out as one of the most precious in the region.

This white-washed village has a rich cultural heritage of which the locals are very proud, and so you'll find it festooned with signposts and information boards. Apart from the Arab castle, the village counts with a Mudéjar-style bell tower and patio in the 16th-century Iglesia de La Encarnación (Incarnation Church), the Roman baths, and the birthplace of Blas Infante.

The Facts

Type:	Circular with a linear part to the summit
Length:	10.14 kilometres
Level:	Moderate
Elevation gain:	697 metres
Time:	4 hours including the summit

What to expect

We can rank this walk among the most beautiful in the Casares region for its far-reaching views over the impressive cliff of Casares and the all-round views from the summit all the way to the coast of Africa. Stunning views will accompany you on most of the walk. The path runs over a long stretch of the grey rugged rocks of the Crestellina mountain, where impressive vultures and eagles add a dramatic touch to the experience.

The first part of the walk goes steeply up a country road which then turns into a more gently ascending dirt road. Half-way you will find the turnoff to the linear part of the walk that goes over a very tricky rocky path leading to the summit Cherro de las Chapas (946 metres). If you want to reach the highest point of this summit, you'll need to climb a bit using your hands. Getting up is easier than getting down, which is to be avoided after rainy days. Once back on the dirt-road circuit, the path continues to the Refugio, where you can have a break at a picnic table. The final part to the village goes down a narrow rocky path, where you have to watch your steps. If you leave out the climb to the summit, you avoid the most difficult part, save about 1.5 hours, and enjoy a rather easy walk. On the other hand, if you want an add-on, there is a small path at the turn just before the Refugio, which goes to another viewpoint. Whichever option you choose, make sure you still have enough energy to walk through the steep village streets.

History, legends and more

Castle

The castle was constructed by the Arabs in the 13th century and was very important due to its geographic position high on a hill top and at the edge of a deep ravine. This allowed it to dominate the landscapes between the coast and the mountains of Ronda. Only ruins of the walls and parts of the Alcázar towers have been preserved. They can be accessed from the town through the gate tower, which also houses an ethno-historic museum.

Julius Caesar

According to legend, Julius Caesar favoured the area and frequented it for the healing power of the sulphurous alkaline waters, which helped him with a skin disease that is said to have plagued him. Folklore associates the horrible smell of sulphur with the last breath of the Devil. Caesar built the Roman baths around the waters, known as the Hedionda Baths, which have become a monument today. Casares was named in honour of Caesar's presence.

Blas Infante

The village is also the birthplace of Blas Infante, who is considered to be the father of Andalucía. He was a famous lawyer, politician, and writer who contributed considerably to the Andalucían identity. Later, he was executed during the Spanish civil war.

Driving directions

Start on the A-7 by the coast, and then turn onto the MA 8300 just before Manilva, passing by the Finca Cortesín hotel. Shortly after entering the higher part of Casares, at the first restaurants, there are fabulous views over Casares village. Parking is available, but at it can get very busy on weekends and holidays. The walk starts and ends in the higher part of the village on the Calle de la Carretera, also designated as the MA-8300.

Step-by-step walking guide

- With the views to your left, walk a few metres on Calle de la Carretera and take the steep climbing country road on the right. There is an information board. The first part follows a tarmac road to the Puerto de las Viñas.

- At a fork, go left onto the wide dirt road and stay on this.

- The next right turn is the entrance to the hike to the summit, if you decide to add this. This is the linear part of the walk that takes you up to the summit on a zigzagging rocky earth path. If you decide not to take this detour, just go straight ahead. It runs along the foot of the Crestellina mountain and is almost flat with amazing views to Casares in the distance and the sea and the Rock of Gibraltar towards the horizon.

- The path goes sharp left towards the nearby Refugio. At this turn, you have the option to walk along the small narrow footpath that zigzags up to a lower mountain top with a beautiful viewpoint. If you decide to include this part, add another 40 minutes to the time indicated above.

- To continue your return, walk on the right side of the Refugio, where you'll find a narrower path with some rocks that zigzags down the slope until you reach a wider country road again.

- Take a right and you'll end up at the Calle de la Carretera again, where you have to turn left. Then keep left to pick up your car or continue your adventure on the right and go down into the steep streets of this white village.

- In the village: make your way down to the Plaza de España, cross this, and walk up to the castle and historical monuments, which are all very clearly signposted and need no further directions.

269

Walk 31: The red Sierra de Bermeja and the unique Spanish fir tree: to the 'Los Reales' peak

The mountain you can see west of Marbella towards Estepona is the Sierra de Bermeja. The peak of los Reales (1,452 metres) dominates the landscape from far away and lends its tints to Marbella's sunset. The mountain is just 10 kilometres from the coast of Estepona, so the town seems squeezed between mountain and sea. The Sierra de Bermeja covers 10 municipalities until reaching the Rio Verde of Istán to the east and Casares to the west. The Sierra Real and the Sierra Palmitera, which you can see around Istán, also belong to the Bermeja mountain range. To the north, it is bordered by the Serrania de Ronda and the chestnut region of the Genal Valley.

It might be hard to believe that this rather obscure mountain has one of the best preserved serpentine ecosystems in the entire world. The serpentine soil contains high amounts of iron and magnesium, which colour it deep red or 'bermejo' (hence name of the mountain). The colour is due to its volcanic origins, when magma started cooling down and minerals on the surface became oxidised. These volcanic rocks, called peridotites, have been extensively exploited in the Sierra Bermeja mountain and also in the Sierra Real a bit further up towards Istán. The soil is challenge to plant growth, but it has given birth to a biodiverse landscape that includes the unique Spanish fir tree or 'pinsapo'. The pinsapo is happy to grow on the peridotite rocks and likes the mild humid conditions high up in the mountain. This tree is said to date back to the Ice Age and it is the only one of its kind that grows on peridotites. Estepona is proud of this rarity and is attempting to protect this natural area for the future by having the mountain range declared as a protected Natural Park.

The Facts

Type:	Circular
Length:	12.28 kilometres
Level:	Moderate
Elevation gain:	502 metres
Time:	3.5 hours

What to expect

This walk takes you to the heart of the red Sierra Bermeja mountain, through the Spanish fir tree forest, and up to the los Reales summit at 1,452 m. Breathtaking panoramic views accompany you on the entire walk, first towards the east coast of Estepona with the Sierra Blanca and inland to the Serrania de Ronda, and, once at the top, towards the west coast, the Valle del Genal, Gibraltar, and Africa. The hike begins lower down at the Puerto de las Peñas Blancas at 1,000 metres and roughly consists of three parts. The first part of the walk runs on an old tarmacked road curving up around the mountain. Then it follows the well-known walks of 'Paseo de los Pinsapos' and 'los Realillos' on rocky forest paths zigzagging up the mountain to the summit with its antennas. Afterwards, it goes back down on a newer tarmacked road—with stunning views to the west coastline of Estepona and Gibraltar—until you

reach the picnic area of the Refugio. You may find yourself above or in clouds because of the nearby Levante winds. This is an extraordinary feeling, especially when it clears up and slowly reveals the spectacular views. But if the cloud is there to stay, watch your steps very carefully and don't get lost!

History, stories and more

La Vuelta

The mountain roads here are a cycling paradise and have to be honoured. Halfway up the mountain drive, at exactly 8.8 kilometres, is the 'Mirador Ciclista' with its sculpture of two cyclists created by the artist Andrés Montesanto. The viewpoint has recently been renovated. The statue is dedicated to the hordes of amateur and professional cyclists who climb this road. For instance, this point marked the end stage of both the 2012 La Vuelta de España and the 2016 La Vuelta de Andalucía cycle races.

Driving directions

Literally begin in the centre of Estepona, on the Avenida de los Reales, which turns into the MA-8301. This road takes you up the mountain towards Jubrique in the direction of Ronda. You drive up until you reach las Peñas Blancas where you turn onto the MA-8304 to Genalguacil. At this point, on your immediate left and behind the open road-barrier, is the old tarmacked road to the Refugio de Los Reales.

Step-by-step walking guide

- The walk starts at the Puerto de Peñas Blancas, the mountain crossing between Estepona, Genalguacil, and Jubrique. Follow the signs 'Los Reales 4.5 kilometres' up an old tarmacked road behind the road barrier with fantastic views on the left.

- Walk up the winding road for about 2.5 kilometres until reaching the start of the hiking path on the right. It's easy to find as there is a signpost with a topographic map indicating the 'Paseo de Los Pinsapos (Pine Tree Walk)'.

- The path is somewhat rocky and goes down through these Spanish Fir trees. It's exciting to see the river flowing after rainy days. After around 15-minutes' walk, you reach a little open area in the middle of the woods called la Plazoleta Genalguacil. There is a tiled plaque inscribed with the poem 'Arboles' (Trees) by the Andalucían author, Federico García Lorca. He was murdered in 1936 at the beginning of the Civil War.

- At this point, you have to turn sharp left up the path that zigzags up towards the summit.

- After the summit, you go down a few metres and go sharp left on the path, which flattens out then gradually climbs towards an antenna. You can sometimes spot griffon vultures here.

- Behind the antenna, the path goes down a tarmacked road that curves back down and passes the Mirador Salvador Guerrero.

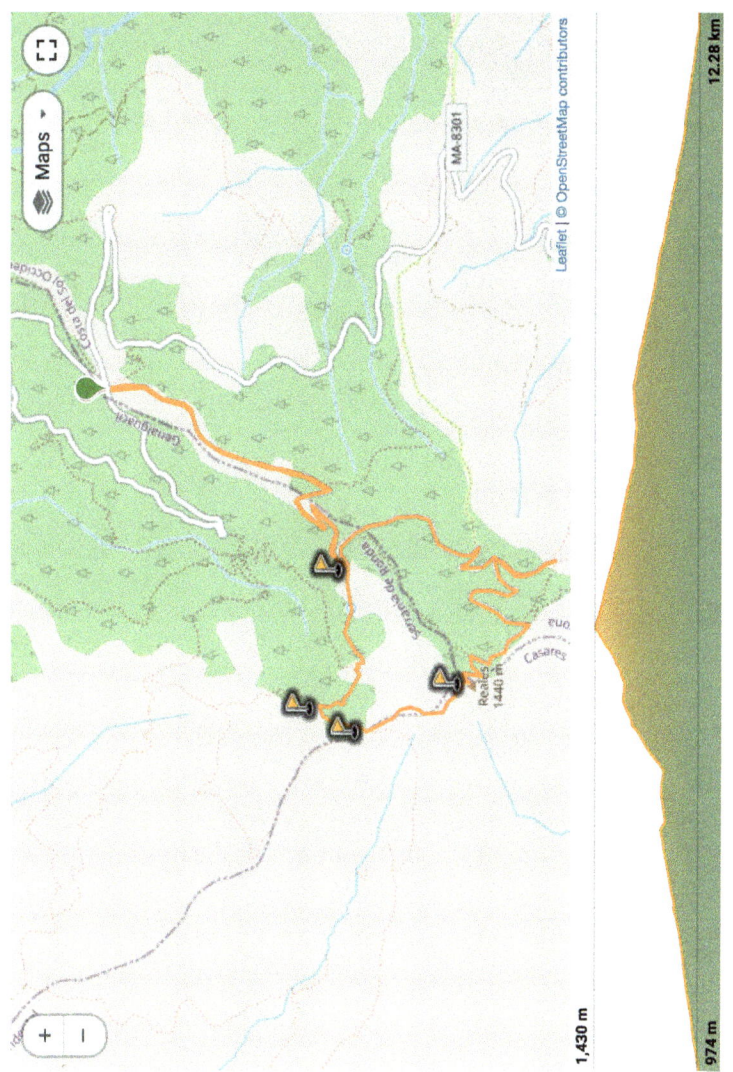

3.3. DIRECTION MÁLAGA-ANTEQUERA

WALK 32: MIJAS PANORAMIC MOUNTAIN CIRCUIT INCLUDING THE 'PUERTO DE MÁLAGA' PEAK

Mijas everywhere

Trying find your way around Mijas can be quite a challenge because there is not just 'one' Mijas. There is 'Mijas Pueblo' on the mountain, 'Mijas Costa' and 'La Cala' on the seafront, and the modern part of 'Las Lagunas'. They total over 149 kilometres2 making it the biggest municipality in Málaga province. Mijas reaps the benefits of proximity to the bustling city of Málaga at only 30 kilometres away. The natural heritage is varied, including protected sand dunes and the Sierra de Mijas, which has a great range of biodiversity. There are many springs on the mountain along with two main rivers, the Río de las Pasadas and the Río de Ojén, which converge in the Río Fuengirola. Challenging walks include the climb to the peak of Puerto de Málaga (1,000 metres) or to the Pico de Mijas (1,150 metres) with its a round white meteorological station called "La Bola", which you can see from far away. The footpaths in the mountains and along the coast are well maintained, and they open windows onto places of cultural and natural interest. These qualities—plus the sun-drenched beaches, teeming restaurants, and golf courses—have recently increased the number of residents to 85,400.

Mijas pueblo welcomes you

The white village of Mijas 'pueblo' is a very popular and well-organised tourist attraction, although it may seem quite isolated at 428 metres on the steep southern slope of the Sierra de Mijas, including the 10-kilometre drive inland. It's busy, hectic, and lively. Mijas knows how to receive and pamper tourists. Once you drive into the village, you are almost automatically guided towards a modern multilevel car park where you can leave your car for the democratic price of 1 euro for the full day. A lift takes you to the top floor and you walk straight into the main square, where you will be welcomed by the tourism office and the proud sculpture of a donkey, which is the village mascot. In front of the office, there's a line of staring braying donkeys and shiny horse carriages offering to give you a tour. There really is something to please all tastes, from attractive souvenir shops and delicious chocolate ateliers to delicious tapas bars and restaurants. There are small unexpected corners and cultural monuments, such as the only oval bullring in Spain (1900), the Parish church (16th century), the sanctuary 'Virgen de la Peña', and even the Mijas Contemporary Art Collection (CAC) with ceramics by Picasso. Every step is a climb up the steep narrow streets of Mijas, but you will be rewarded with spectacular panoramic viewpoints to the Mediterranean. You can also stroll through the gardens and Moorish walls of the ancient 15th-century castle. Starting or finishing up your walk with a visit to the town centre is simply a must.

The Facts

Type:	Circular
Length:	12 kilometres
Level:	Moderate
Elevation gain:	790 metres
Time:	3.5 hours

What to expect

This larger circular route encompasses the three paths with their coloured signposts that run on the southern flank ('la cara sur') of the Sierra de Mijas: the blue 'Puerto de Málaga', the green 'Las Cañadas' and the red 'Cruz de la Misión'. Together they offer the best of views to the entire coastline, the village, inland Málaga, and as far as the Sierra Blanca mountains (Marbella) and the Sierra Bermeja (Estepona). The steep mountain slope guarantees you an intense workout right from the start in the village centre. The first part of the walk, on the rocky blue path, is the most intense with the greatest elevation gain of almost 600 metres. It continues to climb behind the little white chapel in a zigzagging line up to the lower summit of the 'Puerto de Málaga' at 1,000 metres. You pass a big quarry and at the summit you can see the endless hills of inland Málaga. The second part, on the green path, begins by gradually climbing to a viewpoint over the western valley as far as Estepona and 'la Bola de Mijas' higher up. Then the path mainly goes down on the southern flank and into the valley on the western side, where sharply bends onto the red path to return to Mijas pueblo, passing by another quarry. This final part is flatter and gentler. For fans, add 'la Bola' and an extra hour to this walk and you'll have truly seen it all. Be aware that there is very little shade on most of the walk and in winter it can get very cold at the summit.

History, stories and more

In the steps of the monks

The short walk up to the chapel is known as the 'Via Crucis' of Semana Santa (Holy Week). This explains the many iron crosses that decorate the path. The precious one-naved white chapel of the 'Ermita del Calvario' was built in 1710 and visited by the Barefoot Carmelite monks who lived in the monastery in Mijas. They used the hermitage as a place for contemplation and meditation. The Carmelites also excavated a hermitage in the rock, where there was a shrine dedicated to the Virgen de la Peña, the Patron Saint of Mijas. It's now right in the centre just behind the tourism office on the balcony overlooking the hills and coastline.

Sierra de Mijas trees

Only a few minutes' walk from the village centre, you enter an absolutely calm and peaceful oasis. The Sierra de Mijas has a very characteristic look because of the abundance of pine trees that are neatly lined up. This is due to the extensive replantation of pine wood, carobs, and wild olive trees carried out in the middle of the 20th century. The wide spaces between these younger trees expose the greyish colour of the limestone soil and open up far-reaching coastal views at all times.

Rich soil

For centuries, the mining wealth of Mijas attracted many peoples, who actively exploited the mineral-rich soil. For example, Mijas pueblo was founded by the pre-Roman Turdetan people primarily as a small mining village with a fortress. Later on, marble was very popular with the Romans, under whom Mijas experienced a more prosperous period. It was then known as "Tamisa". During Arab rule, Tamisa became Mixa, referring to the numerous mines. In 1487, under the Catholic crown, it was given its current name of Mijas.

Capital of the donkey-taxi

The burro (donkey) is the symbol of Mijas. Their burro-taxi service has become a tradition and a clever tourist attraction. Donkeys carry passengers and their luggage to their hotels or give them a tour around the village. The wellbeing of the cute animals is luckily strictly regulated and regular inspections are conducted by the Refugio de Burrito to look after them.

Driving directions

Take the A-7 towards Málaga and turn onto the A-387 to Mijas pueblo. It's about a half hour's drive from Marbella.

Step-by-step walking guide

- Starting at the donkey sculpture, walk by the beautiful town hall on the Avenida de la Pena.

- Cross this road to make your way up the charming alley 'Pasaje de las Golondrinas' with its 52 steps.

- Pass the local school on the street Cañada Gertrudis and start to climb up a steep foot passage with an information board.

- Cross the road and walk to your left for about 100 metres to find the start of the mountain path on your right. This is the starting point for many walks of varying levels and lengths. We'll follow the blue walk, then the green, and finally the red to find our way back.

- Zigzag up and at the turn go left on the blue path towards the little white chapel, which is a charming point to rest with amazing views towards Mijas and coast.

- Pass the chapel and continue steeply up until a turn, where you go right.

- Angle sharp left up following the blue signpost (don't go straight on, that's the yellow path).

- At the next turn, go right up the path (left goes to the cantera [quarry]).

- At the fork, turn left up the zigzagging path to end on a wider dirt road.

- Turn right on this dirt road and enjoy the views to Mijas and the other side of the mountain. Then leave it and angle sharp left up on a narrow mountain path (don't continue on the dirt road!)

- More views slowly open up to the valley on the right with the quarry.

- At the next turn, go right on the linear part up to the summit of 'Puerto de Málaga'. After enjoying the views inland, you have to trace your steps back to this crossing.

- Leave the blue path, and continue left on the green 'las Cañadas' path, which climbs a little until you reach a viewpoint with the Sierra Blanca and Sierra Bermeja in the distance.

- At the next crossing, keep left and go down. Don't go right, which takes you to la Bola or Pico, unless you want to add this part on.

- Keep left at the next turn (not Fuente de Adelfa). Zigzag down until reaching a wider dirt road.

- At the road, turn right and after a few steps, go the sharp left going down.
- The path gradually becomes sandier and easier to walk on. It runs over the western flank and then goes deeper down into the valley.
- After a long descent, at the turn go straight to Mijas (another 4.3 kilometres).
- Go left 3 times: the third turn goes sharp left towards the quarry.
- Then go down on the right after the quarry. You'll automatically reach the chapel again, which you pass to return to the village square.

WALK 33: CONE-SHAPED ROCK LABYRINTH OF EL TORCAL NATURAL PARK

It's hard to imagine Andalucía was once covered by the sea. Many millions of years later, this left extraordinary landscapes of which El Torcal is one of a kind. El Torcal is an impressive labyrinth of cone-shaped limestone rocks covering more than 2,008 ha. Located between Málaga and Antequera, it is the best kept karst landscape in all Europe. El Torcal consists of the Torcal Bajo, Torcal Alto, Sierra Pelada, and Sierra de la Chimenea, of which the highest peak—Camorro de las Siete Mesas—lies at 1,335 metres.

The Facts

Type:	Circular
Length:	3.5 kilometres
Level:	Easy
Elevation gain:	98 metres
Time:	2 hours

What to expect

To have a good first experience, the park's yellow route is an excellent choice for all levels including children, and can be walked without booking. You will feel as if you have landed on a different planet at El Torcal. The landscape is covered with immense grey cone-shaped rocks. They speak to the imagination and are reminiscent of figurative shapes for which many have received a name, including El Dedo (The Finger), El Camello (The Camel), La Jarra (The Jug), and La Botella (The Bottle).

The first and last section of the yellow route coincides with the green route, which is a smaller circular walk for public use. The walk starts in Torcal Alto at the visitor centre and is very well signposted. However, you should not leave the indicated route as it is very easy to get lost. The path partly runs on flatter areas between the big rocks with wider open views, and partly between corridors with ivy and moss on a narrow rocky path. The walk ends at the Mirador de las Ventanillas (windows) opposite the visitor centre, where you have breath-taking views to the lower hills around the park.

If you are up for a more intense hike, start at the lower entrance and walk your way up on a signposted path of about 3.6 kilometres. This adds another 1.5 hours one-way with an elevation gain of 263 metres.

El Torcal has a mid-mountain climate with fog and northern winds and gets unexpectedly much colder than the coast. After rainy days the rocks get very slippery. You can also book a tour with a guide to walk the Ammonites route, which is not signposted: visit http://www.torcaldeantequera.com.

History, stories and more

Jurassic park

El Torcal was initially formed over 200 million years ago, during the Jurassic period, when a large part of Europe was covered by the Tethys Sea. Shells, carbonate sediments, and fossils of marine animals on the seabed accumulated into horizontal layers that became rocks after millions of years. With the movements of the Iberian zone and African tectonic plates, these sediments compressed, fractured, and emerged from the seabed about 20 million years ago. Meteorological agents, especially rain, ended up eroding the limestone rock, known as karst modelling, which gave shape to the spectacular landscape of El Torcal today. El Torcal was the first natural area to receive national protection in 1929.

Imitative figures

The limestone rock formations inspire the imagination and their figurative shapes have received funny names over time, passed on by people who frequented the mountains in the past, such as shepherds, charcoal burners, and stonemasons. A very representative example is El Tornillo (The Screw)—in front of the visitor centre—or The Camel or The Canary inside the park.

Fauna and Flora

El Torcal is a paradise for birds and has been declared a Zona de Especial Protección para las Aves (ZEPA: Special Protection Area for Birds) by the Spanish authorities. Some birds have become rare here, such as peregrine falcons, Bonelli's eagles, or golden eagles. Others are seen frequently, such as the griffon vultures flying overhead. There are also foxes, weasels, goats, lizards, and snakes, of which the snout viper is poisonous.

An area of El Torcal has been reserved to protect specific plants that grow between the rocks. The long list of plants includes oaks, forest shrubs, blackberry, wild flowers, and an abundance of ivy. There's also the Montpellier Maple tree, which has been incorporated in the Inventory of Singular Trees of Andalucía.

Driving directions

Drive to Málaga and take the AP-46 towards Granada. Leave at exit 115 and follow the curving mountain road, which passes through the village of Villanueva de la Concepción. In the village, turn right at the El Torcal signpost and follow the road until it makes a very sharp left turn. This is the entrance to the lower part of El Torcal. If the upper car park at the information centre is full, they close the barrier and you need to park at the lower area. There is a shuttle bus to take visitors up to the Torcal Alto area. You can also walk there by following the orange route that runs from the lower car park to the Torcal Alto Visitor Centre.

Step-by-step walking guide

- The walk starts at the visitor centre car park, where there is an information board and signposts indicating the green and yellow routes. The walk makes a loop on the west side of the visitor centre. Given the rocks and the similarity of the landscape, it's hard to describe this walk step-by-step. So, it's important to follow the well-indicated route through the natural park or use wikiloc.

- The first part is rather flat, followed by a more uneven passage, where you can try spot the rock figures of The Dromedary, The Canary, and the Sphinx.

- Walk by a Montpellier Maple tree. On its left is an area known as the Castles.

- Cross the green route, which goes left.

- Enter a passage with a hammer-shaped rock.

- Pass the Jug rock and then turn into an alley. Go down towards a sinkhole, where the path goes left.

- Halfway along, the path enters a tunnel surrounded by plants and a

short narrow passage called El Tabaco.

- Then pass through a wider alley called El Burladero.

- From this point there's a little climb up to an open wide alley, where you can glimpse The Camel rock on the right.

- The passage continues upwards to an open area and The Indian rock.

- The circular walk ends at the visitor centre. Continue to the right for 100 metres to enjoy the last bit of this walk, the fabulous viewpoint of Las Ventanillas, which is a window onto the landscape below El Torcal.

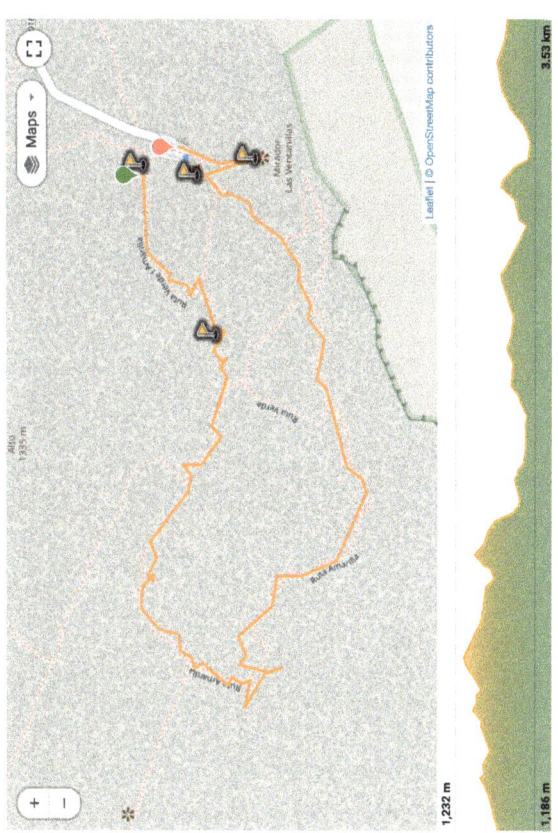

El Chorro: magic water reservoirs, gorge and Caminito del Rey

El Chorro, or officially 'El Parque Natural Desfiladero de los Gaitanes', is an area of outstanding beauty in the heart of Málaga Province, with enormous emerald green reservoirs and a spectacular gorge. And it's only about 50 kilometres from the capital. Three of these magical reservoirs (called 'embalses') meet in El Chorro. The Conde de Guadalhorce reservoir is the first one you encounter as you come from Ardales, whose municipality it belongs to. This is the oldest and was built in 1914. Just a little further along, the Guadalhorce and Guadalteba reservoirs were constructed much later, in 1966, on the rivers of the same name. They are located within the areas of Teba, Campillos, and Antequera. Together with the river Turón, the Guadalhorce and Guadalteba are the three most important rivers in Málaga, converging in El Chorro to form the tail end of the Gaitanejo reservoir. The Guadalhorce river has carved an impressive 3-kilometre canyon in the rocks, reaching heights of 300 metres. At its narrowest, the cliffs are just 10 metres apart. You can pass along the wooden walkway that clings to the vertical cliff-face. This became known as the Caminito del Rey. A walk on this legendary walkway or through the hills or mountains is a breath-taking experience with views that are hard to match anywhere. It is said to be one of the most beautiful landscapes of Spain.

Outdoor paradise

The area is a paradise for outdoor sports of all kinds, like kayaking, fishing, hiking, cycling, and climbing. Climbers from all over the world dare these challenging cliffs and gorges. In recent years, various efforts have been made to stimulate the tourism industry and they have already proven to be very successful. The Great Path of Málaga now runs through the area and more hiking trails have been added, signposted, and documented for all levels. 2015 saw the long-awaited opening of the refurbished Caminito del Rey. Tickets were sold out in the first 6 hours on the online platform. Since then, it has since attracted many thousands of nature lovers from around the globe.

Driving directions

You can get to the area of El Chorro by car in just over an hour from Marbella (from Málaga it's only about 40 kilometres). The most scenic drive from Marbella is through the mountains. You pass Ojén and Monda, head towards Campillos on the A-355, then go the direction of Campillos/Ardales on the A-357. Ignore the first exit to El Chorro/Caminito del Rey, because this would lead you to the south of the gorge and the end of the Caminito del Rey. Continue until the second exit of the Caminito. Just a few minutes after the exit, you can begin to soak up the initial impressive views of the first of the three reservoirs, the immense Guadalhorce embalse. The road zigzags through the green hills by the water. Go straight ahead behind the roundabout (and new visitor centre on the left) until reaching the Mirador restaurant. There's a car park just after the tunnel on the left, or you can park on the road to Gaitanejo.

WALK 34: CAMINITO DEL REY: SPECTACULAR CANYON THRILL

The Facts

Type:	Linear
Length:	6.36 kilometres
Level:	Easy
Elevation gain:	250 metres
Time:	2.5 hours (count 4 hours)

What to expect

Thrill-seeking minds will love the dizzy walkway of the Caminito del Rey (the King's Walk). Of the 2.9 kilometre path, about 1.5 kilometres runs on a narrow 1-meter-wide footbridge pinned to the impressive wall cliffs of El Chorro, 100 metres above ground level. If looking down into the gorge hasn't excited you enough, you can try out the glass-bottomed viewpoint somewhere in the middle of the walk!

Nearer to the south entrance, there's another exciting moment as the path continues on the cliff wall on the other side of the gorge. It's connected by a 100-metre-high hanging bridge 'El Puente de Ribera', which moves a bit when there are stronger winds. But don't worry, it's all very safe and easy for the whole family to walk over (minimum age is 8 years), but it's not recommended for those with a fear of heights. The path is mostly flat, linear, and descends from north to south with a few steep stairs on the last part. In total, this adventure takes around 4 hours, as you need to walk for around 20 minutes through a forest path from the Guadalhorce reservoir along the river to the entrance point. Your walk finishes at the Gaitanejo dam and the old hydroelectric station of El Chorro, where you can catch the next available shuttle bus that drives visitors back up.

You have to book your ticket well in advance because this walk has become a major tourist attraction. Book at: http://www.caminitodelrey.info/. Small groups are allowed to enter at intervals to avoid the path being overcrowded and safety helmets are also provided.

History, stories and more

Death walk

Before it's restoration, the walk wasn't so relaxed and it didn't receive it's name 'the death walk' by chance. In fact, the walk was known among mountaineers as the most dangerous path in the world.

Initially, the passage was built to connect the hydroelectric power plants at El Chorro and Gaitanejo in order to transport materials and inspect and maintain the channel. It was hazardous work done by sailors, who were used to heights. It lasted about 4 years and was completed in 1905. The story goes that prisoners sentenced for life carried out the most dangerous tasks.

Over the years, rust deteriorated the beams and created many gaps, making it extremely dangerous. It became a beloved attraction among extreme climbers in search of the next adrenaline rush. After some fatal accidents, which gave the trail its unfortunate legendary reputation, the walk closed in 2000. Heavy fines were given to anyone daring to venture it.

However, in 2014, expert workers restored the path, which hangs in the air at 105 metres above the river. In March 2015, the safe new path was opened to the public.

King's path

The path received its name of Caminito del Rey after its inauguration in 1921 when the Spanish King Alfonso XIII visited the site. Everyone simply refers to the path now as the 'Caminito'.

Step-by-step walking guide

The walk to the starting point of the Caminito is well signposted. You must arrive at least 30 minutes before your booked entry time as there can be queues at the entrance. You also need an extra 20 minutes to walk to the start.

- The walk starts at the Conde del Guadalhorce reservoir. Walk down the road from the car park next to el Mirador restaurant for about 5 minutes.

- Enter a small tunnel on the right that cuts through the mountain. The tunnel is around 150 metres long and just 2 metres high. A flashlight is recommended as the lights are not always working. Continue for about 100 metres until reaching the dirt road. If you have claustrophobia, you can walk up the road opposite the el Mirador restaurant and avoid the tunnel passage.

- Keep going left and not far away there's a crossing where you go left towards the Caminito entrance, which is at the Gaitanejo reservoir.

- The Caminito faces you right at the start with the 100-metre Gaitanejo gorge above the river. The path runs on the mountain cliff and is almost always flat with some stairs from time to time. The second canyon is the Las Palomas canyon and the third is the Gaitanes gorge or Desfiladero. The hanging bridge and steeper stairs are at the end. After these you can see the new El Chorro Hydroelectric Power Station.

- At the exit of the Caminito, there's a shuttle bus service that takes you back.

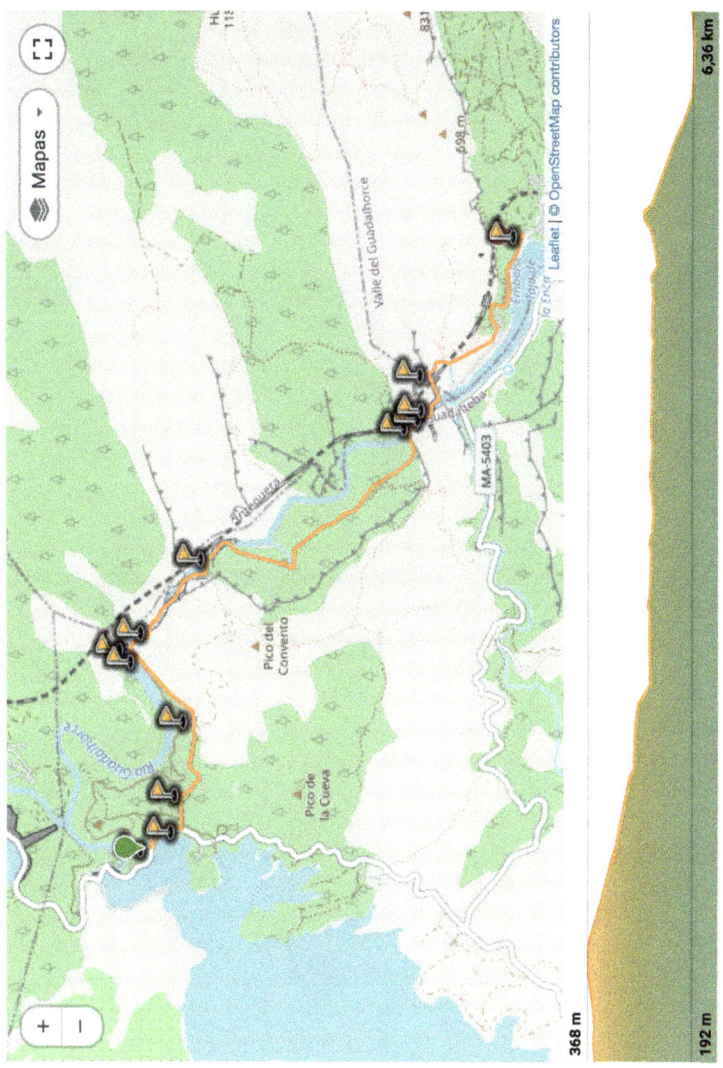

WALK 35: EL CHORRO. LAKE VIEWS' WALK: EL GAITANEJO

The Facts

Type:	Circular
Length:	6 kilometres
Level:	Easy
Elevation gain:	136 metres
Time:	2 hours

What to expect

There's no need to miss out on the fun your friends are having on El Caminito. In the fantastic landscape of El Chorro, this walk is an ideal alternative for those who do not want to do the Caminito del Rey for whatever reason (probably fear of heights!). An easy wide path with little elevation gain runs from the Conde del Guadalhorce reservoir area through the pine tree forest with viewpoints towards the stunning Gaitanejo gorge of the Caminito del Rey and the magical reservoirs. There's a small picnic area about halfway at the Guadalhorce riverside and restaurants at the starting/finishing point. In particular, the Mirador restaurant has amazing views and is an ideal meeting point for both groups, as the return bus journey from the Caminito stops nearby.

History, stories and more

View of the Gorge

You can see the red-beige cliff walls from the Gaitanejo canyon, where the Caminito del Rey path starts.

View of the Guadalteba dam

At the end of the walk, you can see the impressive Guadalteba dam. Its waters join those of the Guadalhorce dam and then with the controlled waters of the Conde de Guadalhorce reservoir. These come together at the tail end of the Gaitanejo reservoir then flow into the Desfiladero de los Gaitanes.

Old bridge view

The decorative architectural arches of the stone bridge have become an industrial heritage of the 20th century. The structure was at the time decisive for the development of the Málaga area.

Step-by-step walking guide

- The starting point is next to the tunnel under the El Mirador restaurant. Walk 550 metres up a gravel road to continue on the signposted Sendero Gaitanejo.

- The path is straightforward to follow (just ignore one right turn). At first, it gradually goes down and then you pass through a tunnel.

- At the entrance to the Caminito del Rey, take the small stairs on the left down to the path by the river. This is called the fishermen's path, which bends sharply back. The path flattens and there's a rest and picnic point at the Pesca stop along the river. You'll pass a beautiful rock with carved lines called 'Arco Gotico'.

- Afterwards, the path gradually zigzags back up and narrows a little through the forest.

- Once up, there are beautiful viewpoints. Go left here to close the circuit and make your way back down to the car park or Mirador restaurant.

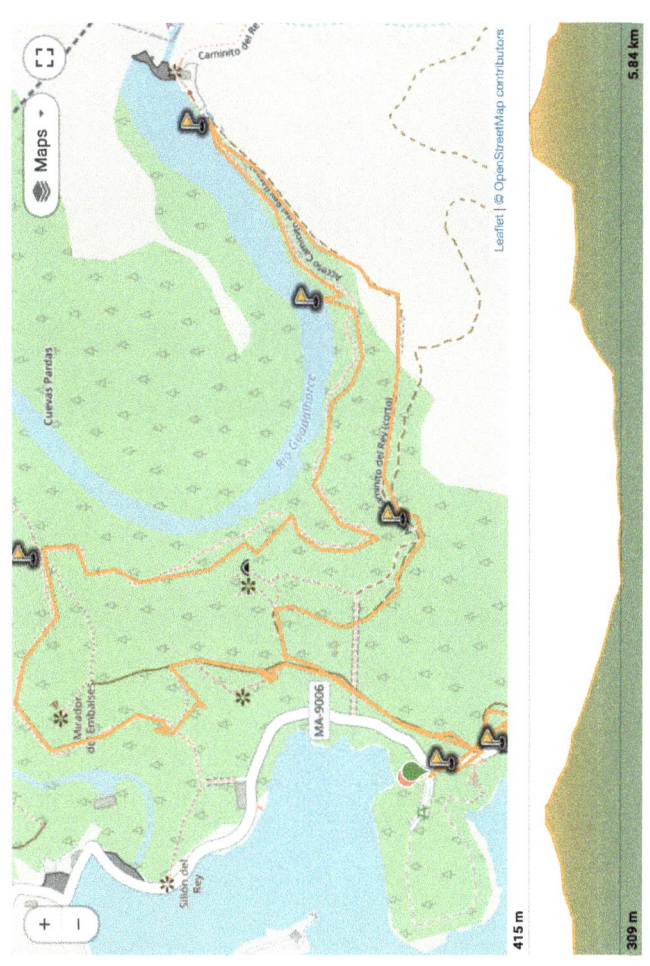

BIBLIOGRAPHY

Online sources

https://www.andalucia.org/

http://caminitodelrey.info

https://www.cilniana.org/hipotesis-sobre-el-entorno-de-la-ermita-de-los-monjes-de-marbella/

https://www.diariosur.es/interior/necesita-acinipo-20181112221032-nt.html

https://www.diariosur.es/marbella-estepona/epoca-gloriosa-miguel-20180421173135-nt.html

https://www.diariosur.es/interior/201610/24/piden-puesta-valor-neveros-20161024005910-v.html

https://www.diariosur.es/marbella-estepona/201412/12/pedro-inaugura-bulevar-pone-20141211235237.html

https://www.diariosur.es/opinion/estado-cuestion-castano-20190208000901-ntvo.html

https://www.elmundo.es/viajes/espana/2021/02/04/601a9f42fc6c8304188b45b8.html

https://www.elrefugiodelburrito.com

https://www.euroweeklynews.com/2015/09/03/a-monster-masterpiece-lives-in-puerto-banus/

https://www.eyeonspain.com/blogs/luislopezcortijo/19372/a-sauce-with-a-lot-of-history-in-southern-spain.aspx

http://grupos.us.es/puertosandaluces/pdf/Ficha_Marbella.pdf

http://www.juntadeandalucia.es/cultura/archivos_html/sites/default/contenidos/archivos/ahpmalaga/documentos/DocMes201807_Refugiojuanar.pdf

https://www.juntadeandalucia.es/cultura/agendaculturaldeandalucia/evento/acinipo-visitas

https://www.juntadeandalucia.es/cultura/enclaves/enclave-arqueologico-acinipo

https://www.laopiniondemalaga.es/

https://www.malagahoy.es/ronda/Sierra-Nieves-joya-verde-Parque-Nacional_0_1534046768.html

https://www.marbellaactiva.es/wp-content/uploads/2013/04/Ver-articulo-El-Camino-de-los-Monjes.pdf

https://www.marbellaclub.com/es

https://www.malaga.es/

http://museobandolero.org/historia.htm

https://www.nytimes.com

https://www.puenteromano.com

http://www.rurality.com/whattodo/ardales_es/embalse-guadalhorce-guadalteba/tosee

http://www.sendalitoral.es/

https://www.sierrabermeja.es

http://www.surinenglish.com/

http://www.sierrabermeja.es

http://www.sierranieves.com/imagenes/planosierranieves.pdf

https://www.theolivepress.es/

http://www.torcaldeantequera.com/

https://www.andalucia.es/

https://vegadelmar.org

Municipalities websites

http://www.ardales.es/es/Turismo/Naturaleza/Embalses/Espacios_Naturales/

http://www.benahavis.es

http://www.benaojan.es

http://www.cartajima.es
http://www.casares.es
http://www.genalguacil.es
http://www.grazalema.es
http://www.istan.es
https://www.marbella.es/
http://www.monda.es
http://www.ojen.es
https://www.setenildelasbodegas.es/es/
https://turismo.mijas.es/

Magazines

El Caminito del Rey, Hiking & Trekking magazine, Breda, 2015.

Books

Alcalá Marín F., *Crónica de Marbella. Historias, tradiciones, leyendas y algunas cosas más*, Malaga, 2006.

Amador, J.I., Tobaja, *El Chorro. Paraje Natural: Desfiladero de los Gaitanes*, Arguval, Malaga

Becerra Parra, M., *Parque Natural Sierra de Grazalema. Guía del Excursionista*, La Serrania, Ronda, 2012.

Bishop T. and E.M. Bratek, *Walking in the Ronda mountains. 30 half-days walks in Andalucia*, La Serranía, Ronda, 2011.

Gómez-Alarcón, J.A., *Guía de la Sierra de Mijas*, Malaga, 2006

González, M.R., *Visitors´guide. Reserva ecoloógica dunas de Marbella*, Marbella, 2019.

Mata, A.M., *Un Hombre para una ciudad*, Ricardo Soriano, Marbella, 2005.

Serranía de Ronda, La Serranía, Ronda, 2006.

Sánchez Sánchez, A.J., *Parque Natural Los Alcornocales. Guía del Excursionista*, La Serranía, Ronda, 2015.

Navarro Carrillo, D., *Guía de la Vereda del Faro*, Malaga, 2010.

www.ingramcontent.com/pod-product-compliance
Lightning Source LLC
Chambersburg PA
CBHW061252230426
43665CB00026B/2913